CONTENTS

ACKNOWLEDGEMENTS

Thanks first of all to Andy Saunders at *Management Today* for commissioning the original 'Don't You Believe It' column. Thanks also to Andy and his colleagues Matthew Gwyther and Emma de Vita for their assistance in turning the columns into a book.

Thanks to Andy Bass for being the ideal collaborator, and to Itamar Levy and Nick Temple for psychological insight. Thank you to Robert Kirby at United Agents for helping to secure publication with John Moseley at Headline Publishing.

And, finally, thanks to Sara for more blessings than I can list.

INTRODUCTION

Imagine a high-stakes poker game. In the course of the session, millions of dollars will change hands. All the players have read the same books, understand the same systems, know perfectly how to calculate the odds in any situation, and over the course of the game will receive the same mix of good and bad cards. And yet, it's the same few players who win consistently. What gives them the edge?

The same question applies in business. Globalisation means that more and more we will all have access to the same markets and the same supplier base. Via the web, we have access to the same information, and the same ideas from the same business schools. Where do we find our edge, our competitive advantage?

Whether you are a poker player, the CEO of a huge global corporation, a one-person business or a corporate employee developing your own career, sustainable competitive advantage comes from the same place. *Inside your own head.* Poker players know that the way to win consistently at the the high-stakes tables is to have a better understanding of psychology, your own and your opponents', than anyone else. The same holds true in business, but it hasn't been as widely understood.

This is your chance to get ahead of the game. I hope you'll take it.

CHAPTER 1

WHY WE GET STUCK, AND HOW TO BREAK OUT

WHY DOES DOING THE RIGHT THING FEEL SO WRONG?

It's a puzzle. We look at the world, and see so many things being done that don't make sense. This book is full of them. For more than two years I have been writing the 'Don't You Believe It' column for *Management Today*. Each month I find a new piece of conventional wisdom or accepted practice to disagree with. I used to worry that I would run out of things to take issue with, but it doesn't happen. And let's be honest, it's not just others who do these daft things. It's me and you. We can apply logic, we can look at examples and see different, better ways of doing things. And yet, we resist.

Later in the book we are going to meet, among others:

- ▶ The group who almost closed their operation in one country before realising that it was, in fact, a growth opportunity
- ▶ The sales manager working hard on ways of reducing his sales forecast
- ▶ Incentive schemes that encourage and reward worse performance
- ▶ Pricing strategies that make absolutely no sense at all, yet increase revenues

And that's before I think about all the daft things I have done in my own life, or the things you have done in yours – be honest.

There's an objection forming in your mind already. How can this possibly be true? If so many of us are making mistakes in so many areas, and if I claim that they are so obvious, why has it been going on for so long? It's not because we're stupid. It's because we spend so much time thinking about how to make and do cool new things, we don't spend the time thinking about thinking. That's the promise of this book. We can be *dramatically* more effective at what we do. We don't need to become more intelligent, learn a whole new range of skills, work harder, or acquire vast amounts of extra knowledge. When it comes to knowledge, skill and intelligence we have what we need. The improvement comes from upgrading our thinking about the way we use what we already have.

This is why I am starting this book, a book about the popular misconceptions in business and how to avoid them, by talking about the Caveman Brain.

MEET THE CAVEMAN BRAIN

Do you remember the old days, when we lived by hunting and gathering, when death by sabre-toothed tiger was an occupational hazard, and we used to get very excited about the new season's fashions in bearskin wraps?

No, neither do I. But parts of our brain do. Life in the Stone Age may well have been nasty, brutish and (usually) short, but it was simple. Risks and opportunities were few in number, easy to spot, and it wasn't hard to work out what to do about them.

Imagine there's a more advanced civilization at the other end of the galaxy, who discovered us five millennia ago. They send someone to check in on us once every thousand years or so. This year's visitor would note the progress we have made in technology. The houses we live in, the tools we use, and the amount of information available to us have all developed almost beyond recognition since the last visit a thousand years ago. Our intergalactic visitor would certainly approve of, could even be impressed by, our progress in these areas. On the other hand, they would be dismayed by the way we think our way through this new world we have created. So often we seem to be stuck in the Stone Age, applying caveman thinking to information age issues.

We need to think more about our thinking, the aliens would conclude, or we're going to get into a serious mess.

In fact, it's the Caveman Brain that is causing most of the thinking problems described above, thanks to its two guiding principles.

Caveman Brain Principle 1 – Familiarity is Security

Think of the poor caveman put in an unfamiliar situation: say, transported from the savannah to the jungle. Everything's different – the flora, the fauna, the sights, the sounds, the smells. How is he to tell what is safe and what is dangerous? It's very hard. He lacks experience of this new environment, but also lacks many of the other skills which we would use to decide whether we were safe or not. He doesn't have any science to help him work out what is safe to eat. He has no books written by people who have been there before who can tell him what they found out. When it comes to thinking things through for himself, he is handicapped by a primitive language and no education which might help him to use logic.

It's a difficult problem, one that the caveman solves in the only way available to him. He takes refuge in a very simple maxim – 'familiarity = security'. Or, put another way, 'If this situation is familiar, it means I have survived it before and so can survive it again. If it's unfamiliar, I'm not taking the risk.'

For a primitive man in a primitive world, this is an excellent strategy. It works well because it doesn't demand much in the way of intelligence, reasoning power or knowledge, but also because the conditions of the primitive world were simple. As a simple method for unsophisticated people in straightforward circumstances, it's brilliant. It's not hard to understand why those individuals who operated this strategy tended to survive longer. They lived longer, had more children and so passed the strategy on through the generations to us, encoded in our brains.

The problem arises when the world is no longer simple. The maxim 'familiar = safe' is very useful when the world is basically unchanging. Change, however, has a way of making the familiar obsolete, and hence unsafe. Consider the US car makers through the 1960s and 1970s. Ford, Chrysler and General Motors competed vigorously with each other, but all produced very similar, large, gas-guzzling cars. On the one hand it felt like a ruthlessly competitive world, but on the other it felt very familiar, and therefore safe. Disaster struck with the arrival of the Japanese on the global car manufacturing scene. They had very different ideas about cars, and the American car-buying public found them very appealing. According to research conducted at Cranfield University, Japanese manufacturers' market share rose from a minimal 5% in 1970 to 20% by 1980. The US manufacturers were slow to respond – even a couple of years ago a commentator on the crisis in the industry commented that they seemed to find it hard to produce the cars that people wanted to buy.

Change will make the familiar unsafe. This is not a problem that the caveman had to deal with, but it is endemic today. Intellectually, this is not a hard proposition to accept, but there's part of the mind that finds it really hard to deal with. That part is the Caveman Brain, and when it is in control it's very hard to counter. It's not amenable to argument – how can you argue with something that's basically primeval? The symptoms of Caveman Brain are powerful but hard to pin down; if you experience its power at all, it expresses itself as a feeling of discomfort, an inexplicable reluctance, even inability, to do what seems eminently sensible. Often you don't even realise that

Caveman Brain is operating; it blinds you to unfamiliar possibilities, or to the risk of the familiar.

Caveman Brain Principle 2 – Social Conformity

Imagine it's the early 1950s and you are an undergraduate at Swarthmore College, Pennsylvania. You have volunteered to help Professor Solomon Asch as an experimental subject in a study of spatial perception. You and a group of seven others are in a room with the professor. He puts up a slide of the diagram below, and asks the group, one by one, to look at the line on the left and say which of the three lines on the right is the same length.

The first person says 'Line C'
The second person says 'Line C'
The third person says 'Line C'
The fourth person says 'Line C'
The fifth person says 'Line C'
The sixth person says 'Line C'
The seventh person says 'Line C'

Now it's your turn to answer. It's obvious to you that the correct answer is B, but all seven people before you have said C. What are you going to say?

Actually, you've been tricked. You are the only real subject in the room. The experiment isn't about spatial perception, but about social conformity. The other seven people are in fact colleagues of the professor, deliberately giving the wrong answer in an attempt to manipulate you. In the real experiment, 75% of people went along with the crowd.

The experiment shows that it's really hard to do the obvious, sensible thing when everyone else is doing something different. This same point was established in a much, much more elaborate and expensive experiment in the banking industry over the last few years.

It's not hard to see how this approach to social conformity would have benefited a band of primitive people. In a simple, unchanging environment the group view probably is the right one. When you are living close to the subsistence level it doesn't make a lot of sense to spend time debating issues, particularly since 'debate' in that sort of society was probably more likely to involve weapons than carefully developed arguments.

The real experiment relied on an number of collaborators deliberately misleading the subject. This isn't necessary for the mechanism to operate. Think of the fairytale of the 'Emperor's New Clothes'. Here there was a tacit agreement that it was easier to maintain the fantasy than to speak the truth – i.e., let's all pretend that the emperor is beautifully clothed. This might have worked in the fairytale, but imagine the results in a clothing business operating in a competitive market.

The same mechanism of group-think can operate in real life. The Slovenian philosopher Renata Salecl described a startling discovery made in her country after the end of communism. Many people had lost faith in Communist rule, but laboured under the impression that the majority still believed, and so kept quiet. Only when the Communists were swept from power did it become apparent that almost nobody still believed in communism, not even the apparatchiks who ran the country. This large majority of disbelievers, however, had all believed that they were in the minority and so kept quiet.

Poor old caveman. The world has moved on, and continues to move. He just can't deal with it, but he isn't going to go away. He occupies a very old, primitive part of the mind. Upgrading our think-ing isn't going to be easy, but there are things to be done. The first thing to do is to spot the traps so as to avoid them.

THINKING TRAPS

It's important to understand how you are thinking, and to be able to choose the right method for the right issue, but that's only half the battle. There are some fairly predictable traps, or ways in which our Stone Age heritage not only conditions the way we think, but prevents us acting on our conclusions even when we get it right.

Thinking Trap 1 – Magical Thinking

This is very popular these days. Go into any bookshop and head for the 'self-help' section – it is so big now that it's hard to miss. Here are shelves full of guaranteed recipes for success, wealth, love ... The cynic might ask why instructions on how to succeed in the really big, important areas of life seem mostly to be simpler than the instructions on how to program your DVD recorder.

The cynic (and in this area I am a cynic) might further remark that while you can clearly market a book with a title such as *Six Steps to Get You the Life You Want*, nobody is going to buy a book called *The Six Moves Guaranteed to Win Any Chess Game*. Anybody who knows anything about chess would laugh at such a book. There's no best move – it all depends on what stage of the game you're at, where the pieces are on the board and who your opponent is.

The cynic's final shot might be to ask why, if it's all so easy, are so many people clearly so unfulfilled, to the point where they need to keep buying the books? A really good self-help author would in fact shoot themselves in the foot: i.e., write one book that solves everybody's problem, and thereby put an end to the whole industry. But leave aside the question of efficacy; what are these books telling us?

There seem to be two main strands:

❶ If you want it enough, visualise it enough, it will come to you. The best example of this is Rhonda Byrne's *The Secret*.

❷ Alternatively, if that seems a bit flaky, you might enjoy the willpower school more. Here it is just a question of will; if you aren't getting what you want, it's because you have chosen not to get it. Want it enough, work hard enough, and you will have what you want.

Magical thinking crops up surprisingly often in business:

▶ A new mission statement will get us moving again (the power of visualisation, even if we have no evidence that the mission is attainable, or any idea of what's got to be done, or changed, to bring it about).

▶ Stronger incentives (bigger carrots for top management, bigger sticks for the workers). The might of willpower. Want it enough, and you can make it happen. You don't need to spend too much time thinking about what you are going to do, or why what you have been doing hasn't been producing the results you want, or why, if what you have been doing hasn't been producing the results, doing more of it will improve matters.

The appeal of magical thinking is that it relieves us of a lot of thought, and a lot of uncertainty. Willpower trumps cunning, or planning. You don't need to plan – just set off with enough energy and optimism and it will all come right.

This form of magical thinking very cleverly defends itself from attacks. If you tried it and it didn't work, there is an answer ready. You clearly didn't follow the recipe closely enough, or you just didn't believe enough, or try hard enough. It's your fault – don't shoot the messenger.

It's not hard to see how this sort of thinking appeals to the caveman. For a primitive person, magic is real. In the absence of science and any logic to examine cause and effect, we took refuge in superstition and ritual. What else could you do? Magical thinking is particularly appealing when you feel uncertain or confused. It simplifies matters, and is always presented with great confidence. You are being invited to put your destiny in the hands of a higher power – just follow the steps, do what you're told and somehow somebody or something will make sure that it all comes out all right for you. It's what a psychoanalyst would call a 'dependant fantasy'.

Like it or not, things have moved on. It's time for a reality-based approach to our aspirations. Any time you feel yourself drawn to a 'guaranteed recipe' or 'six points that cannot fail' you are succumbing to the charms of magical thinking. When you can't give a clear story about cause and effect, magical thinking might be taking over. Practise spotting it, in yourself or others, and avoid at all costs.

Thinking Trap 2 – Status Quo Bias

This isn't an irrational liking for a timeless rock band, but a systematic flaw in the way we think about risk.

We do think about risk, but to have any chance of dealing with it effectively we need to distinguish two different types:

Type 1

The risk arising from doing something. 'Doing something' could be anything from asking someone for a date to using advanced technology to drill for oil in the Gulf of Mexico. Type 1 risk feels risky. Whatever it is, when we decide to do something, we are conscious of the risk involved, even if we aren't particularly good at assessing its severity or planning how to manage it.

Type 2

On the other hand, we tend to be much less conscious of type 2 risk; i.e., the risk arising from *not* doing something. We might not ask for that date, and miss the chance of a wonderful relationship, or we might not develop that new product or approach and doom our company to failure. Curiously enough, however hard we might try to conjure up a vision of the regret and lost opportunity arising from our decision not to take action, that vision seems so much less vivid and less compelling than the visions of failure which present themselves when we do act. The strange thing is that type 2 risk often feels safe.

Consider how different approaches to risk conditions how we take business decisions. I once worked in an internal consultancy unit of a large group which owned, among other things, a group of theme parks. One day the Group Finance Director asked us to review and comment on an investment proposal from the flagship park. They wanted to spend a very large amount on a new roller-coaster ride – bigger, faster and scarier than anything previously seen.

There was an interesting divergence of opinion when it came to the financial business case; not as to its merits as an investment case, but more fundamentally about how to assess it. One view was that this was a big investment decision, and needed to be assessed as such. If we spend the money, will we make enough back to justify the investment?

The other point of view was different. It saw the new rollercoaster not as an investment, but as a cost of staying in business. If you want to maintain your position as the UK's leading theme park, then at least every other year you need to offer the public something new that is bigger, faster and scarier than anything seen before. The question then was not 'should we do it?' but 'how do we afford it?'

There was merit in both points of view, but they were approaching the question from completely different angles. The first was focused on type 1 risk – what happens if we do this thing? The second point of view was focused on type 2 risk – what happens if we don't?

There is a very strong bias towards type 1 risk, with an implicit assumption that the status quo is always an option. Doing nothing much may not be the most exciting or profitable course of action, but it's always an acceptable one. For the caveman, this makes perfect sense. 'The future, unless I do something to change it, will remain like the past. I have survived the past, so that is fine.' Again, what has changed is *change*. The status quo is no longer an option and your present comfortable, familiar platform is likely to be eroded by technological progress, demographic changes, globalisation or the efforts of your competitors.

Thinking Trap 3 – Isolation

When we look at a situation and try to decide what to do, a perennial risk is to focus too narrowly. This can happen at any level, as the following examples show:

- A software company had difficulty collecting amounts due from customers. The issue was that the problem had been defined as poor performance from the finance department, whereas in fact the finance department couldn't do much without the collaboration of the software development, professional services and legal departments. When these people were brought in, the problem was solved rapidly.
- A company making plans assuming that competitors won't respond, whereas in fact they of course will.
- It seems mobile phone manufacturer Nokia recently fell victim to isolated thinking. They had for many years been hugely successful making handsets based on the Symbian operating system. Then the market changed fundamentally. The advent of the smartphone, whether

Apple or Android, meant that the handset was no longer a discrete piece of equipment but the centre of an 'ecosystem' of applications and other services produced or supplied by a huge range of third parties. Symbian just couldn't support this, and Nokia were slow to recognise the problem. In the end, to obtain a viable operating system, they did a deal with Microsoft, a distant third in the market.

Thinking Trap 4 – General Risk Aversion

I was once asked to give a speech to a trade association on the subject 'Is There Risk in Publishing?' I almost suspected that they hoped I would tell them that there wasn't, and they would all have gone home happy.

Of course I told them no such thing, but gave them a fairly academic half hour on how to identify risk and deal with it. If I'd had the same request today, my answer would have been much brisker. It would have been something along the lines of:

'Is there risk in publishing? Of course there is. Business without risk would be like cooking without salt, or life without sex. Risk is just another word for possibility. Accept that it has this dual nature, and embrace it. That's all I have to say. Now go back to work and do something great.'

We tend to overestimate risk, again thanks to the caveman. Think of the caveman as someone up to his chin in water. There was no safety margin in his life. One false move, bad decision, poor harvest or hard winter and he's dead. In his world, risks with even relatively small consequences are fatal. Add to this the status quo bias previously mentioned, and it's clear why the caveman is very risk averse.

Of course the world has changed. Most of the time we have a safety margin – we can afford to experiment and absorb the costs of unsuccessful experiments. In fact, we *have* to experiment because the status quo probably isn't an option.

Thinking Trap 5 – The Fundamental Attribution Error

This one is so common that social psychologists have invented a special name for it. It is defined on Wikipedia as 'the tendency to overvalue dispositional or personality-based explanations for the observed behaviours of others while under-valuing situational explanations for those behaviours'. In plainer language, we could say that when people do things that we don't like we tend to explain it in terms like 'That's just how they are' rather than 'That's what you would expect given the situation they are in.' Chapter 7 on incentives gives examples of this. The purchasing manager ordering four years' worth of stock wasn't doing it because she was stupid and didn't understand the importance of cashflow, but because her objectives required her to do so. The credit controllers in the software company were failing not because they were lazy or useless, but because the organisation didn't give them access to the people who could solve the problems.

It's clear that getting to grips with this one could make a huge difference to your effectiveness as a manager. Fortunately the social psychologists offer some techniques for doing just that:

❶ Take a 'consensus' view. If most people in a given situation behave in a particular way, assume that it is the result of the situation, not the individuals' dispositions.

❷ Ask yourself how *you* would behave in the situation.

❸ Look for hidden causes, like the effect of incentive structures and organisational structure.

So that's the nub of it. Systematic problems with thinking lead to systematic problems with behaviour and therefore performance and results. The following chapters range over many different areas and identify a weird and wonderful range of errors that spring from patterns of thinking that have gone awry.

After a thorough examination of some common problems that arise from sloppy thinking, I am going to offer some solutions. Part of the answer lies in better thinking tools, and part in improved thinking, which means understanding more about your own thought pattens and the ways in which emotions, often primitive emotions, condition what we see and do. The penultimate chapter offers a range of thinking tools to overcome bias, rescue us from the thinking traps and produce better decisions leading to more effective actions. Then the final chapter will give you ways of dealing with the emotional side of your mind, to be sure that doing the right thing feels, if not right, at least less wrong.

CHAPTER 2

PRICING

PRICING SHOULD BE BASED ON COST OF PRODUCTION

This is a really, really bad idea, as we shall see. However, even if it were a good idea, it would be impossible to implement. Trying to use it would drag you into a mass of confusion and contradiction.To understand why, consider this story. It is one of many making the same point, but I think it makes it particularly powerfully. It may even be true.

One day in Paris a wealthy woman goes into a café, and sees Picasso. After a few minutes, she summons up the courage to approach him. 'Monsieur Picasso,' she asks, 'would you make a portrait of me? I'll pay you anything you want.' Picasso nods, grabs a menu and in five minutes has sketched the woman's portrait on the back of it. He hands it to her.

'Five thousand francs,' he says.

'But Monsieur Picasso, it only took you five minutes.'

'No, madam, it took me my whole life.'

You don't have to be a famous artist for this to happen. A company I know provides very large databases of scientific information. One day it was approached by one of its largest clients, a global pharmaceutical company. They wanted a customised interface. The company determined that this would take twelve days of programming time. They quoted a fee, which the client accepted. How much was the fee? One million pounds.

Are these prices high, or are they low? Let's say you wanted to set prices based on the amount of time needed to do the work. What is that time? Picasso is absolutely right to insist that it's not the time taken to do that particular task, but the time taken to get to the point where you can do that task. In Picasso's case, that was his whole life. For the database company, again, the cost of being able to build the customised interface isn't just the programming work, but the cost of assembling the database and, crucially, coding it in a way that made it easy to build the interface. This cost was something like a hundred highly qualified people working for twenty years. This made one million pounds look like a bargain, just as five thousand francs for the benefit of Picasso's life's work is low.

This is also the reason why I, as a consultant, try to avoid billing clients based on a daily rate. Like most knowledge workers, I have spent years learning how to do what I do. On one occasion, I gave a ten-minute talk to a group, as a result of which one member, with no further help from me, changed something in his business to raise his income by 10% the next month and every month after that. How would I price that? As five minutes' worth of work? Or according to the weeks and months I spent studying the subject matter? Should I also include the time I spent practising to be a good speaker, so that he was actually paying attention to what I said? (The thing I told him about, by the way, was to use a differentiated pricing scheme, so pay attention to this chapter and it could make a significant difference to your profit margin.)

There's one other thing as well. Like most other knowledge workers, I do a lot of my best work when I'm thinking about something else, or even when I'm asleep. If a problem is perplexing me, I try to forget about it, take my son to the park, have dinner and then go to bed. When I wake up in the morning, the solution has become obvious. This is normal operating procedure for people who are in the business of solving hard problems, but it does create an interesting issue for time-based billing. You want me to bill you for time spent? Simple. The clock starts at our first meeting, and continues 24 hours a day until we conclude the project. And by the way, since a lot of the work is going on in the unconscious mind, which can deal with several things in parallel, it's quite legitimate for me to charge my other clients for the same 24 hours a day, seven days a week. If that's acceptable to you, I'll happily bill you by the hour.

OK, you say, I accept that pricing based on the cost of production doesn't work when 'production' is basically hours of brainpower. But what about physical stuff, i.e., goods, not services? Sorry, cost-plus pricing doesn't work there either.

Consider an aircraft engine. It takes lots of complex materials and many hours of manual labour to put it together. But the true cost isn't in the materials or the labour. Interestingly, the cost is in the design, *but the real value is in the knowledge*. What does this mean? Obviously, there is value in the design. There are plenty of companies who could produce bits of metal, plastic or rubber to a blueprint, but only two companies in the world, Rolls-Royce and GE, who know how to design large aero engines. Interestingly, though, that is only part of the story. I had a fascinating conversation with someone from Rolls-Royce, on the subject of intellectual property protection. Could someone steal your engine design? I asked. Yes they could, he replied, but it wouldn't do them any good. There are people who could disassemble an engine and make an exact copy, but it wouldn't fly. In fact, bits of it would melt, or break. There are things you need to know about materials science that you can't work out from the engine itself. It's not enough to have a complete blueprint – you need to know how to make it. It's the same story – the value in the engine is inseparable from Rolls-Royce's sixty-year history of making engines.

So, I'm arguing that, even for physical stuff, the value is really in the knowledge that went into creating it, not the actual cost of making the thing, and that therefore it makes no sense to base pricing on the cost of production. But wait, you say, I'm cheating. For my example of stuff, I'm taking the aero engine, a very advanced technological product. What about more ordinary things?

All right, what about training shoes and sportswear? Is that 'ordinary' enough for you? Look at this market. Stuff carrying a brand name, like Nike, sells for more than a product of the same quality from a lesser brand, or a product with no brand, despite quite possibly coming from the same factory and being made of the same materials. It's a slightly different version of the same story – the *cost of selling the product includes a lot of cost incurred before the thing is made.* For the consultant or the artist, the cost is the time taken to learn to do what they do. For the aero engine manufacturer, it is decades of research and development. For the sportswear manufacturer, it is marketing and branding.

HOW COST-PLUS PRICING WILL DESTROY YOUR BUSINESS

Just in case you are still tempted to find a way to make cost-plus pricing make sense, consider this.

I did some work with a European engineering company which makes components for hydraulic equipment. Sometimes their customers just want components, but other times they also want engineering expertise. The customers are trying to design a system with a particular capacity or response time that might need to fit into an awkward space. They can't work out how to do this, but my client's engineers can.

In the UK, the engineering company priced these projects on the basis of cost plus a mark-up, achieving a gross profit of around 30%.

In Italy, they used a different approach. It wasn't a formula, it was a process. Specifically, the process was: 'Let's all get in a huddle and think of a number.' It worked very well – on projects where the company was contributing significant expertise to solve tricky problems, the Italians could achieve margins of 70% where the British would settle for 30%. I've no reason for supposing that the Italians were more capable engineers than the Brits – they just had a better sense of the value of their expertise.

There is another twist to this story as well. In the UK, the engineering company was struggling to maintain profitability (hardly surprising, you might say, if they were using such a poor pricing model). To boost profits they were looking for new sources of materials – China rather than France, and Romania rather than Germany. This was reducing costs, but can you see the trap they were walking into? Operating a cost-plus pricing system, every €100 they saved on materials resulted in a €130 reduction in prices. They were literally cost-saving their way out of business.

Interestingly, I have told this story and asked the question – 'Can you see the trap?' – of hundreds of managers at meetings of trade associations and chief executive groups, and at most only 1 in 20 has seen it.

PRICING SCHEMES SHOULD MAKE SENSE

No they shouldn't. Logical consistency isn't a good attribute of pricing schemes. Psychological consistency is, and that's very different. Consider this example reported by the behavioural economist Dan Ariely (in a lecture he gave at 'The Entertainment Gathering', Monterey, California, December 2008, which is viewable on YouTube).

He noticed this advertisement for subscriptions to *The Economist* (see the first example overleaf).

Now what is the sense of this? Why would anyone take the print-only subscription when they could take print plus online subscription for the same amount?

He tried some experiments with his students.

First, he offered them a choice between the three options, and noted the market share (see the second example below).

Online subscription	$59
Print subscription	$129
Print and online subscription	$129

So nobody took the 'stupid' option. He removed it, and noted the market shares again (see example overleaf).

Everything has changed! Previously the more expensive choice was overwhelmingly popular, but now more than two-thirds went for the cheapest option. All because of the presence or absence of an obviously stupid option that nobody chose.

Now if you are the economist Adam Smith, or any of his intellectual descendants who like (need?) to believe in 'rational economic actors', you will be tearing your hair out at this point. If, on the other hand, you approach the question psychologically, it makes perfect sense.

Offer	Price	Market Share
Online subscription	$59	16%
Print subscription	$129	0%
Print and online	$129	84%

Offer	Price	Market Share
Online subscription	$59	68%
Print and online	$129	32%

This is the psychological logic: it's really hard to assess value. How can you decide whether $59 is a good deal for one year's worth of online subscription to *The Economist*, or $129 for print and online? What do you compare it with? That is where the stupid option helps. The stupid option makes the $129 print and online option, the most expensive, *look like good value*.

You have now arrived at an existential moment. You can either deplore the absence of rationality in economic life, or you can embrace it and profit from it. If the former, throw this book away and take a job as an economist in a university or, better still, a bank. If the latter, read on, as there is much more to delight and enrich you.

PRICING SHOULD BE CONSISTENT

Why? It only makes sense for different customers to pay the same if the value they receive is the same. That is usually not the case. Value varies enormously. Suppose, for example, you are a global bank. You receive two pitches from software vendors.

The first goes:

'You have a problem with matching confirmations in your back office. A significant proportion of transactions which should be handled automatically get rejected and have to be resolved manually. Our product will reduce the reject rate from 5% to 1%, thereby saving you £1m per annum in back office costs.'

The second goes:

'As global head of operations, you are responsible for regulatory reporting to seventeen different bodies across the world. The reports have to be on time, and they have to be right. If you mess up, you will be closed down, as happened to a top tier bank in Japan recently. You currently have a problem. You have six different databases which are supposed to agree to each other, but don't. You have seventeen people seconded from internal audit frantically trying to tie things up while you lie through your teeth to all sorts of people, praying that you can clean up the mess before you get found out. Our product will save you.'

Of course, in both cases it's the same product. The product may be the same, but the value to the organisation is very different. Why would you charge the same amount?

Whatever you charge, it's a lot less than the 'cost' of the product – in this case, an average of thirty developers working over ten years.

In this case, the difference in value is real. In other cases, it might be perceived.

Years ago, I was Commercial Director of a marketing consultancy and noticed a very strange anomaly. We did 'medical communications', which meant we helped big pharmaceutical companies launch new drugs. We had scientists who could analyse clinical trial results and spot how to develop marketing messages from them, messages which could be scientifically supported. We charged clients on a fixed price per project basis and achieved, on average, £150 for every hour we spent on a project. Then we added a 'professional relations' arm. This was a rather different but complementary range of services. It was less about hard science and more about helping the pharmaceutical companies develop relationships with the key doctors and academics – i.e., the 'opinion leaders'.

The two parts of the business did different things, but

there was one area of overlap. Both had an 'advisory board'. This involved bringing together a dozen or so top specialists from around the world and getting them to discuss the client's product. It produced useful information for the client, and increased awareness of the product among important clinicians. The pricing was very odd.

When it was done as part of a 'medical communications programme' it was priced on a project basis, and made around £150 per hour. When it was done by the 'professional relations' people it was based on hours spent and hourly rates, which made us about £100 per hour. Note that the hourly rate basis was effectively a fixed fee – if we went over the budgeted hours the client wouldn't pay for the extra.

How could it be that the same activity delivered by the same company could cost the client 50% more or less depending on how it was labelled and which department did it? Even more interesting, the anomaly seemed to cause more concern within the company than it did amongst the clients. I remember agonised internal discussions, but I don't remember any comments or complaints from clients.

In the case of medical communications and professional relations, we are dealing with a customised product which offers obvious scope for differentiated pricing. In today's internet-enabled, information-rich, friction-free world there shouldn't be any scope for this sort of price differentiation when it comes to goods which are essentially the same in all markets. That's the theory, but nobody seems to have explained it to the markets. Take a business to business example, and a consumer example.

The Swiss subsidiary of one of my clients sells engineering components both to Original Equipment Manufacturers (OEMs, who make machinery to sell on to others) and manufacturers, who use the machines for their own production. As a matter of routine, they charge the OEMs 25% more for the same range as the manufacturers. It makes no sense, but it works.

Recently I was looking for an electronic piano for my son to learn on. I went to eBay, probably the ultimate low-cost, highly efficient, customer friendly market. I found something that seemed to fit the bill. I noticed that it was sold by a music shop in Cardiff. I wanted to read a little more about the piano, so I found their website, and was intrigued to see that the piano was priced there at about 10% more than the price offered on eBay.

This sort of thing shouldn't happen these days, and it would be prudent to assume that it will become more difficult for companies to operate differentiated pricing models. Nevertheless, don't assume that you can't still do it. Even if increased transparency makes it harder and harder to maintain these price differentials, it just means that you will have to raise your game. The component manufacturer could offer a different level of service or warranties (that doesn't necessarily cost them any more) to the OEMs. Or the piano seller could create an eBay version with a different model number and reduced functionality (disabling some functions, or leaving them in and just not telling anyone about them).

DIFFERENTIATED PRICING IS SNEAKY

You may feel that differentiated pricing is sneaky, or in some way dishonest. The fact that it's also called price discrimination doesn't help – 'discrimination' isn't a nice word. On the other hand, you could just take the view that if customers are buying they must be happy, and if you're making more money that's only to the good. If you're in the second camp, you can skip this section. If you're in the first, let an economist's explanation reveal why price discrimination is in fact a good thing – or 'increases welfare' in the jargon.

Look at the standard economist's demand curve:

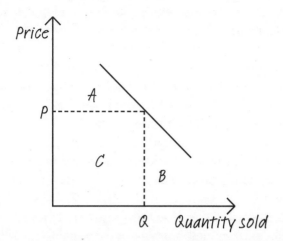

If you have to make all sales at the same price, there is one price that produces the highest possible profit. This is marked *P* on the chart, and it results in quantity sold of *Q*. The total amount of money you receive is *P* times *Q*, which is the area marked *C* on the diagram.

The area *A* represents money that you are leaving on the table. It's the money that the higher-paying customers would have paid, had you set the price higher.

Area *B* represents lost sales. These are customers who would have bought if the price had been lower. They would have been profitable at that lower price. The problem is that lowering the price would have cost you more in terms of lower prices to existing customers than it would have made you in extra sales.

If you could find a way of charging more to the higher-paying customers and less to the lower-paying customers, treating your customers more as individuals, then your revenues go up, but in addition more customers get what they want.

Imagine what would happen in the airline business if there was a rule that everyone had to pay the same, all the time, for a particular route. This would be a big problem for airlines, who are currently charging business class customers more than leisure travellers, or charging more for peak periods than quiet periods, and more for late bookings than for bookings made far in advance.

Under a single price regime, the route may become unviable. There could be no single price at which the airline can make an adequate profit. The price is either too high, and there aren't enough passengers, or it's too low, and they don't pay enough. The service stops.

So price discrimination isn't some horrid exploitative strategy. It's a way of making possible business which simply wouldn't be possible if everybody had to pay the same price.

The good news is that there are many, many ways of managing differentiated prices. We'll come to them later.

YOU HAVE TO MATCH THE COMPETITION ON PRICE

This is the road to ruin. Once you have decided that you are going to be the same as everyone else, but cheaper, you have doomed your business. Competitors do the same, and profitability is driven down to the bare minimum required for survival. Then some idiot takes prices down to the point where they lose money, and people start to go out of business. Be realistic: if the only thing which differentiates you from your competitors is price, then you have turned yourself into a commodity and you will never enjoy the returns you need to grow the business, to devise new products or develop your staff.

There is only one exception to this rule. It makes sense to be the cheapest if you also have the lowest costs. This doesn't mean being good at controlling costs. It means something much more profound. To understand what, look at the archetypal successful low-price, low-cost player: the airline Ryanair. They have been hugely successful in dragging fares down to levels where only they can make money. Look at how they have done it:

- They fly to the cheapest airports. If a destination has more than one airport, Ryanair will always choose the cheapest, which is usually the one furthest from the city centre.
- They standardise. Until recently, they only operated one type of plane, which reduces maintenance costs.
- They are large compared with most of their competitors. Smaller low-cost airlines have come and gone, while Ryanair goes from strength to strength. This has a lot to do with their size, and corresponding buying power and economies of scale.
- They educate their customers to behave in ways that lower their costs. We would prefer you to check in online, because that lowers our costs, so we will charge you extra to check in at the airport. We'd prefer not to pay the airport for baggage handling, so we will charge you to check in baggage. In-flight catering costs money, so if you want to eat or drink in flight, you pay for it. This is not the conventional airline approach to customer service.
- They target a particular segment of the market. Someone who travels by Ryanair is someone who wants to pay as little as possible, and is prepared to give up a lot in order to do so. This isn't the whole market. The banker travelling at short notice between the City of London and Frankfurt, a lucrative passenger for another carrier, is not going to consider Ryanair.
- They build a culture focused relentlessly on cost. The original low-cost airline model was developed by Southwest Airlines in the US. Their CEO, Herb Kelleher, used to say that it was very easy to take a decision at Southwest. Simply ask: 'Does doing this help make us the cheapest carrier between X and Y?'

It's obvious that a low-cost strategy can work, but you need to be able to meet some criteria:

- ● Be large, or become large very quickly.
- ● Build a company culture which values cheapness above all else.
- ● Ignore those customers who value service, convenience or feel good factor.
- ● Probably most importantly, find a big enough market of people who care only about price. This doesn't mean buyers who ask for a discount (they all do) or who would prefer to pay less if they could (they all would), but buyers who demonstrate by what they do, not what they say, that they will sacrifice other things for a low price.

If you can tick these boxes, you may have a chance. There are risks, however. Strategy guru Michael Porter helpfully lists them in his book *Competitive Strategy* (1980), and I have paraphrased them below:

- ● You're making a big bet that you can be better than any competitor when it comes to designing low-cost processes. If you're wrong, you're in big trouble.
- ● You may be able to take the existing process and run it more cheaply than anyone else, but you may be caught out by changes in technology. If someone else comes up with a new, cheaper way of doing things, again you're in trouble.
- ● If you are trying to serve a large market, there may be competitors whose focus is narrower. If they are more specialised, they can pick off part of your market, optimise for that and produce more cheaply for that segment. If a number of people do this in different parts of your market, they can substantially reduce the possibilities for you. This is serious, because to be cheap you have to be big, remember?

As well as these risks, remember that there is room for only one cheapest provider in a market. If you have more than one contender for that title, competition can be based only on price, and the results can be a bloody price war.

Given all this, it's obvious why, for most businesses, competing on price is at best a recipe for a lifetime of unprofitable struggle, with returns depressed to the bare minimum. At worst, it could be the road to ruin, as so many low-cost airlines have discovered recently.

MORE EXPENSIVE OFFERINGS NEED TO BE PRICED HIGHER

No they don't. One of the delightful quirks of pricing is that it can actually make sense to spend money to degrade your product. Here are a couple of examples.

At one time, IBM sold a laser printer to the corporate market. It cost $1,000 and printed at ten pages per minute. Then they launched a version for the small office/home office ('Soho') market. This sold for $500, and printed at five pages per minute. The only difference between the two products was that the slower version had an extra line in its software which commanded the printer to wait.

This seems perverse under normal economics, but looked at in the light of pricing logic it is brilliant. Once IBM have designed the machine and built the production line, they can produce extra copies of the machine very cheaply – it's just a collection of metal and plastic bits, after all. They can make money selling it for $500 to the Soho market, provided they can still sell it to the corporate market for $1,000. However clever they are, they can't just offer the machine at different prices in different markets, because the corporate buyers will be on to them in a matter of weeks. Then all sales will be at $500 and IBM won't make enough to cover their development costs.

The solution to this puzzle, and the way in which IBM could have their cake and eat it, was to develop a lower-value version; five pages per minute just wasn't good enough for the corporate market.

So What Do You Do About Pricing?

It should be quite clear by now that pricing is a psychological minefield or, to my mind, a wonderful playground. It's hard to see which of the parties is more illogical; is it the buyers with their weird behaviour when it comes to making choices, or the majority of sellers with their unhelpful ideas about value, cost and consistency? The caveman (discussed in Chapter 1) is completely out of his depth here, which promises a major opportunity for anyone who is prepared to go beyond the obvious.

THE KEY TO REALLY EFFECTIVE PRICING

In two sentences, the key to effective pricing is this:

> *Imagine that you dealt with every customer as an individual, and knew exactly how much they valued any possible version of your offering, and that the price charged to any customer remained unknown to all the others. Develop a pricing scheme which gets as close as possible to this ideal.*

You are trying to avoid two types of leakage:

- ▶ A customer who values you very highly buys at the same price as everyone else. They would have paid more – you have left money on the table.
- ▶ A customer who puts a low value on your offering doesn't buy at the price you charge everyone else. They would have been profitable at a lower price, but you couldn't find a way of offering it to them without other customers migrating to that lower price point.

Another way to look at it is by way of a diagram:

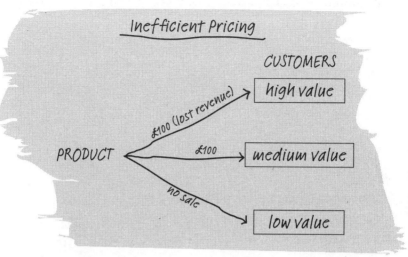

Think whether you are more likely to find additional revenues above your present price point, or below it. It will depend on the business you are in. Consultancies or technology firms who solve difficult one-off problems are more likely to generate additional revenues by charging more for truly valuable work, while hotels and airlines are very good at making money from the bottom of the pyramid – the people who are happy to book at the last minute or travel off-peak but who, in the absence of a really cheap deal, wouldn't go at all.

Next, think about whether the value you offer is created when you provide the goods or the service, or whether it comes from the work you have done prior to that moment. This is particularly important if you see potential in higher-value offerings. If you are a consultant, or a manufacturer of hi-tech equipment, you may be able to solve in moments a problem which has perplexed your customer for years. You can do this because of the years you have spent learning to do what you do. That is the value that you deliver to the customer, and that is what you need to be paid for. It has nothing to do with how long it takes you to assess that particular situation and make a recommendation, or the cost of materials and assembly that go into your product.

Next, decide how much you can segment your market:

❶ Can you deal with customers as individuals? This is the obvious choice for consultancies or designers of bespoke software solutions, but it can work well for simpler services as well. It could for instance be applied by personal trainers or garden maintenance companies. What is most important is that customers are sufficiently few in number and large enough in value for it to be worth the time taken to develop a personalised offering.

❷ If you can't deal with customers as individuals, think about dividing them into different groups, each of which has a different idea about value. Airlines do this when they offer alternate fares to business and leisure travellers (keeping the business travellers away from the leisure fares by requiring a stay over a Saturday night).

❸ If you can't see logical groups, apply the Starbucks solution – offer three choices and let the customers segregate themselves.

Now you are ready to work out how to approach your market.

If you deal with your customers as individuals, it's a question of understanding the true value of what you provide. This probably means talking more with the customer to understand exactly what their challenges are and how you contribute towards meeting them. Look at this as a win-win process; you may well be able to charge more for what you already doing – and that's quite fair if you are delivering value – but the real potential comes from finding additional ways to help the customer. They may be buying components, and struggling to find ways to make them into a functioning system. Perhaps you could help them.

If you have so many customers that you need to deal with them in groups, you need to determine the groups, and then find ways to offer different versions to the different groups. Here are some examples, with alternate ways of segregating the market.

- ▶ Different levels of urgency. For example, online providers of stock price information see different markets. One market is traders, who need absolutely up to the minute information, and pay very highly for it. The other is people who are more casually interested, or want to track the performance of their portfolio every few days. For these people, the data providers license information to websites at much lower prices. This data is always delayed by at least 15 minutes so that it is no use to the traders. The book trade uses the same approach. The hardback edition costs twice as much as the paperback, not because it costs twice as much as the paperback, but because there is a certain market who will pay £15 or so for a novel because they want it as soon as possible. Then there's a larger market who are prepared to wait for the paperback.
- ▶ Different levels of performance. Like the IBM laser printers described earlier; ten pages per minute for $1,000, five pages per minute for $500.
- ▶ Different levels of quality. Stock photo agencies use this approach. Someone needing an image for a glossy brochure needs a higher-resolution image and is making a larger investment than someone using the same image on a web page. The higher-resolution image is therefore more expensive. Note that the cost to the agency is higher for the low-resolution image – the image is provided in high resolution and further steps are needed to produce the lower-resolution version.

Finally, if you can't divide your market up into meaningful groups in this way, offer options, just as Starbucks offers everything in three sizes. Three is a very good number for deep psychological reasons. There is research showing that if you start with two options, regular and large, and add a third, extra large, you will increase sales *even if nobody buys the extra large option.* Customers will migrate from regular to large, because large isn't large any more. Large is now medium, and most people feel most comfortable in the middle. It is the principle of aversion to extremes or, more colloquially, the Goldilocks principle, after the little girl in the fairy story who ate the porridge which was not too hot, not too cold, but just right.

Once you have implemented your Goldilocks scheme, pay careful attention to the proportions in which people buy. If lots of customers go for the largest of the three, introduce another, even larger version. If everyone is taking the smallest, you are probably still losing people at the bottom so introduce an even smaller version.

Treat all these new pricing ideas as experiments. Be prepared to modify them in the light of experience. Notice that some approaches, such as offering a higher-value option in addition to the existing offering, are risk-free. You cannot lose sales (the way you could if you raised all prices) – the worst that can happen is that nobody buys the higher-value option.

PITFALLS TO PREPARE FOR

Some people find the principles here easy and intuitive. They quickly get to grips with them to increase their profits and satisfy more customers. Others struggle, or feel themselves rebelling. If you are in the latter group, it's worth having a good talk with your inner caveman. Here are some ways in which Stone Age thinking traps could be holding you back.

❶ 'It's harder than my existing approach.' Yes it is. Thinking about how customers differ from each other, how they value your offering and how to reflect that in what you do is hard mental work. Console yourself with the thought that it's probably some of the most valuable mental work you could do in your business. A lot of this is uncertainty avoidance.

❷ 'It's risky. You want me to set prices based on what I think my customers think? Sounds very dodgy. I'll probably get it wrong.' More uncertainty avoidance. Yes, you will get it wrong. It's called experimentation. There are ways to contain the risk. If you don't feel comfortable raising prices, try to identify the customers who really value your offering and offer them a premium version. Then the worst that can happen is that nobody takes it, and you learn something useful. Or implement a Goldlilocks pricing scheme with your existing offering as the smallest option.

❸ 'Raising prices will cost me customers.' This is a reflex reaction. You are probably suffering from status quo bias. Remember that if your existing pricing scheme doesn't follow the principles described here, it is probably costing you money. You are losing the opportunity to serve lower-value customers, and leaving money on the table with the high-value ones.

CHAPTER 3

COST CUTTING

COST CUTTING IS A GOOD WAY TO BOOST PROFITS

When profits are low, cost cutting seems to be a popular strategy. For some, it is almost the only strategy. But wait. It may well not be the right thing. Even if it is, there are still many ways to get it wrong. Let's stop and think.

Here is the basic thought process:

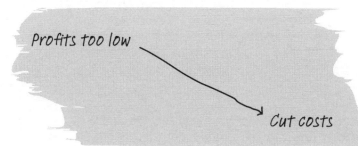

This has the merit of simplicity, but it's Stone Age thinking. It comes from the same part of the brain that our ancestors used when, walking through the dark forest, they were confronted by a sabre-toothed tiger. It went: 'Big, scary animal – lots of teeth – fight or flight – decide *now*.' In fact, our Stone Age ancestors were being more sophisticated than the cost-cutters; at least the brighter ones, the ones who survived long enough to reproduce and become our ancestors, considered two options. Let's honour that inheritance and use the thinking power we've developed since then.

Here's the full picture. Remember the most important point – you don't want to cut costs. You want to improve profits. Cost cutting is just one of the options to consider.

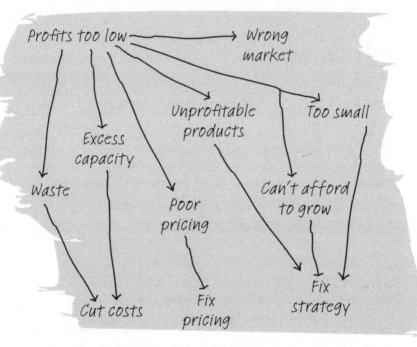

OK, this is a rather more complicated picture than the previous one. On the other hand, compared to, say, programming your DVD recorder, it's still quite simple. Now we can see that there are seven possible diagnoses, two of which lead to a prescription of cost reduction and five of which lead elsewhere. Let's go through them and look at how to tell if they are part of the problem, and how to deal with them. First of all though, let me give you an invaluable piece of advice.

Mike's ROI Rule

If your eyes are beginning to glaze over, you have my permission to skip the rest of the chapter, so long as you read this section.

I met Mike about ten years ago. He was (still is) a private equity investor, and I was Finance Director of one of his companies. He came to every board meeting, and usually sat very quietly, until someone said that we needed to spend some money.

'Any money you spend is an investment decision,' he would remind us. 'It doesn't matter whether it's in the budget, or whether you spent it last year, or whether Fred has resigned and you need to recruit a replacement at the same level. The only reason for spending money is because it produces a return on investment, that's to say you get back more than you spend.'

Apply this rule and you will be in the top 10%. Sometimes it will tell you to cut costs more drastic-ally than you ever would have thought. At other times, it will tell you to spend more, because it will produce more.

Bear this rule in mind as we move through the different areas.

Waste

Business people love waste – it gives the idea that they can boost profits with some simple, uncontroversial moves. It was a popular line in the 2010 general election campaign as well – reduce the deficit without nasty cuts to services or tax increases by reducing waste in the public sector. This didn't convince many people – as one newspaper commentator remarked: 'At least one unrealistic claim will be made tomorrow by the chancellor of the exchequer, Alistair Darling. He will say that swingeing cuts in the public sector need not damage frontline services. The reason is the tooth fairy. She alights each night on his pillow and turns £11bn of cuts into £11bn of efficiency savings. This fairy is now the patron saint of politics.'

So is it possible to make a major impact on business performance by reducing waste? There are examples, but it's telling that I have had to go back quite a long time to find one. It's the late, great Arnold Weinstock of GEC.

Through the 1950s and 60s, Weinstock built an empire by acquiring slackly run companies and, among other things, eliminating waste. The trouble was – that was then, and this is now. One of his acquisitions maintained a large warehouse just off the Strand, right in the middle of central London. Even by the standards of the time this was pretty daft, but that sort of opportunity for improvement just doesn't exist any more. Even by the 1980s it was hard. By then GEC was highly successful, in fact famous for owning a massive pile of cash. The shareholders, however, would have preferred it to invest the money in growth, but GEC seemed to have run out of ideas. Perhaps there just wasn't that much waste to eliminate any more.

These days waste, if it's still there, is pretty well entrenched. Look, for example, at British Airways, currently wrestling with the fact that, for historic reasons, they pay their cabin crew up to twice as much as their low-cost rivals do. Obvious waste, but not easy to deal with. The company can argue that their salaries are way out of line by present-day standards, but remember that the staff have built their lives on the assumption that they can earn these salaries until they retire. They won't give up without a fight, and could do BA serious and permanent damage in the process.

Management has a valid point, but may not get its way. A radio pundit, asked what BA Chief Executive Willie Walsh would be doing to prepare for the strikes, gave a very interesting answer: 'He should be spending a lot of time with his share-holders, because they may be starting to think that Walsh is the problem.'

You'll have worked out by now that I'm a waste sceptic. In fact I see it rather like housework. Dirt (or waste) is constantly creeping up on you, and you are constantly cleaning it up. It makes your house a more pleasant place to live, but no amount of cleaning, scrubbing, hoovering or polishing is going to turn your three-bedroom semi into Buckingham Palace.

Excess Capacity

This is more interesting. In some businesses it's easy to spot whether you have excess capacity. If you're a professional service firm you will have everybody filling in timesheets and so will know whether you have enough work to keep everybody busy. If you're a taxi driver you will know if you're spending too much time waiting at a taxi rank or cruising around looking for a fare, rather than driving with a passenger in the back and the meter running. In many other areas, though, excess capacity can be harder to spot, and the opportunity therefore greater.

Let me give you a couple of examples.

I was Commercial Director of a marketing consultancy, part of a large listed publishing group. My company had started life as a publishing company before evolving into a consultancy. Given its publishing heritage, nobody really paid attention to the question: what is the relationship between the level of revenue and the number of people employed? Once I asked the question, I found that it wasn't too hard to answer. Three rather startling facts emerged:

- We had 25% more people than we needed to deliver the level of work we had.
- In spite of that, everyone seemed really busy all the time.
- In spite of that, we were making very good profits.

This created a dilemma for me; did I mention to the group that we enjoyed such ample staffing? I decided not to, but to make sure that the problem worked itself out over time through growth and natural wastage. If I had told them, we would probably have been instructed to lose some people, which would not have been fun, and could well have caused real problems. Although we had more people than we needed, everyone was always very busy, when necessary with pointless activity. We had to get rid of the pointless activity in order to deliver the client projects with the right number of people. I preferred that we did this in our own time.

You may not approve of my approach here, but let me assure you that it's very common in large organisations. So long as the results come out all right, nobody will own up to spare capacity. Many won't even realise it's there. The better ones will at least identify it and decide privately to do something about it. This behaviour is the logical consequence of the incentive structure in many organisations, and understanding this has made me a very effective poacher turned gamekeeper. I have a nose for excess capacity, and can sniff it out even where it's invisible to those running the business, as in the next example. It would be worth your while developing the same skill. Here's another example to help do just that.

A specialist printing business used many different processes to print in many different ways onto all sorts of different things. A major contributor to costs, if not necessarily to revenues, was a set of big Heidelberg litho presses. Here was an obvious area to ask the question about capacity – a big fixed cost, staffed 24 hours a day. The Finance Director became a bit suspicious about utilisation – every time he saw these mighty beasts, they were lying idle. However, this wasn't evidence. He couldn't stand by the machines 24 hours a day for a month, but was there a way of proving or disproving his suspicion? It turned out that there was. It was very easy to find out how many sheets of paper had been used in the past month.

Making a few assumptions about the size of jobs and the speed at which the things ran, it became clear that they were operating at between one-third and one-half capacity. The irony was that the head of department was getting very excited about getting Heidelberg to increase the speed from 10,000 to 12,000 sheets per hour. In fact, he could have closed down half of the presses or run them at half speed and still got all the work out of the door on time.

It can be quite hard to assess how close to full capacity

everything is, but there are reasonableness checks to be done. Work out the activity rate, and compare it with other benchmarks if you can find them. Even if you can't find external comparators, it can be revealing just to see what's going on. Here are some data from a study of an engineering company in Spain, with comments:

❶ Salesmen handle 40 key accounts each – *surely* they can manage more than that?

❷ Customer service staff process 25 order lines each per day – probably not bad, given that they often need to advise on the exact component needed and 20% of the time need to order the part needed from another supplier.

❸ Three warehouse staff pick and pack 75 order lines (25 shipments) per day – quite good, bearing in mind that they also assemble parts and do maintenance work, while maintaining a very fast service.

The comments are totally unscientific, based on nothing but intuition. Nevertheless, they do offer a way forward. There's no point in benchmarking points 1 and 3, as 1 is obviously too low, and 3 is almost certainly OK. I can concentrate on examining 2, and trying to find some external comparators.

The bottom line on excess capacity: it can exist in a substantial way, and offer a worthwhile cost reduction opportunity. The harder it is to quantify utilisation, the less reporting you have on it, the bigger the opportunity.

Before you start collecting masses of new data, use a little cunning. Be 'hypothesis-driven'. This is consultant-speak for having a suspicious mind, developing hypotheses by intuition and being creative in finding the information to confirm or deny them. Don't expect anyone to tell you about the existence of excess capacity. Even if it's staring them in the face, they may not have noticed it. Even if they have, they won't own up to it.

Poor Pricing

Or, pricing that will make you poor. Pricing offers many, many opportunities to improve profitability, many of them much easier, faster and lower risk than trying to reduce costs. That's why we have had a whole chapter on it earlier in the book. The most important thing to do is to abandon cost-plus pricing and think very hard about value. If profitability is slipping, it may be because customers' ideas about value are changing. If that is the case, you must understand how they are changing, and adjust yoru approach accordingly.

The second thing to do with pricing is to make sure that you have it under control. I once worked with a magazine company who had completely lost control of the pricing of advertising. They had told the sales force to get volume, and they had responded with an orgy of discounting. They were selling pages at 20% of the rate of some of their competitors – that is to say that for the price of one page in a competitor publication, they would give you five. It's particularly easy to get into this mess when times are hard and customers are putting the pressure on. Resist, or regret it for years.

Action Points on Pricing

When times are hard, you must:

❶ *Ruthlessly control pricing* – moving control up one level in the hierarchy, say from sales rep to sales manager, or sales manager to sales director, or sales director to finance director, could be a good move – and *face down pricing pressure.*

❷ *Disconnect pricing from costs* – or else you will give away all your hard-earned cost savings.

You Can't Afford to Invest

Here we come to one of the most insidious risks of cost reduction. Here you can succumb to illusion, produce apparently great results but permanently harm the business.

To see this illustrated on a grand scale, let's look at the achievements of another great British industrialist, Lord Hanson. I have less admiration for Hanson than I do for Weinstock. Weinstock's empire was based on solid foundations but came to an end because his successors gambled it away on grandiose ventures in telecoms. Hanson's on the other hand was built on sand and succumbed, inevitably, to its own contradictions. It's probably the best example of this for the past 100 years.

One of the main things Hanson looked for when identifying acquisition targets was the opportunity to reduce costs. If the target company's capital expenditure was greater than its depreciation, that is to say it was buying new plant or equipment faster than the existing stuff was wearing out, that was interesting. If it was spending a lot on research and development, that was good, because it meant that Hanson could reduce that spending to boost profits. Lavish headquarters buildings were also a good sign.

From one point of view, all these things are the same – opportunities to reduce costs and thereby boost profits. From another, more intelligent, point of view, however, they are fundamentally different. Moving to a cheaper location or getting rid of the corporate jet is just a cost saving. Reducing capital expenditure or research and development is sacrificing the future of the company to the immediate short term.

The story of Berec, the maker of Ever Ready batteries (remember them?), is instructive. Hanson bought Berec at a time when technical change in the battery industry was speeding up, and the business was becoming more international. They ignored both of these trends, instead running the business for short-term profit before selling it. The new owners reported that they found it 'a number of years behind the times . . . a business in decline . . . the whole infrastructure was pretty thin . . .'

So Hanson was actually 'harvesting' – acquiring what others had built up and turning it into cash. This is what this approach would look like:

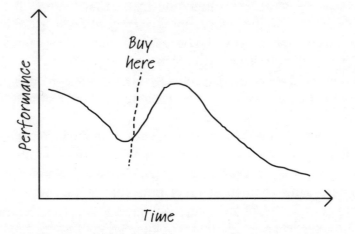

The Hanson trick

At the start, everything looks wonderful. Then things start to decline. If you are an acquisitive conglomerate, though, you can fix the problem with a new acquisition:

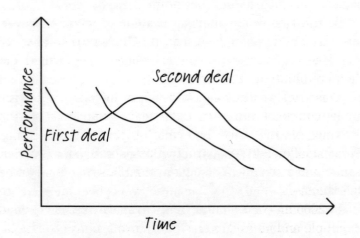

The Hanson trick – step 2

After a few years, of course, you run into the same problem, and so need a third acquisition:

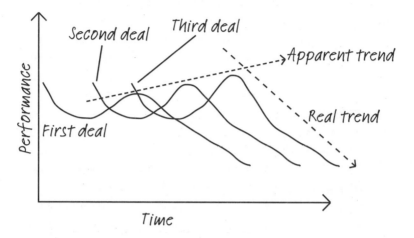

The Hanson trick – step 3 to step N

After a while, the same problem recurs, so you make a fourth acquisition . . . but now you see the real problem. You have created a Ponzi scheme, a little like Bernie Madoff. You have to keep making bigger and bigger acquisitions just to keep the show on the road.

This happened to Hanson in 1991 when they tried to buy ICI. There was no logic to this, no credible story of how Hanson could improve this business. They failed and their credibility never recovered.

This trick works best, and works longest, if you are a big conglomerate with charismatic management, the backing of the City and murky financial reporting. For a smaller company, the implosion will come sooner. Sometimes it may be worse than an implosion – it might be an explosion.

In 2005 an explosion at BP's Texas City refinery killed 15 people and injured over 170. An investigation by the US Government Chemical Safety Board found antiquated equipment, corroded pipes about to burst, and safety alarms that didn't work. The Chairman of the Board drew a direct link between this alarming situation and BP's mandate to the plant managers to cut fixed costs by 25%.

It is, thankfully, unlikely that your business could kill anybody through its unwillingness to spend for the future. It could easily kill revenues, though. A consultancy found this out, very painfully. It had a first-quarter review meeting with the parent company. Sales were materialising slowly, and profit was behind budget. It had budgeted to increase the sales force, but hadn't managed to complete the recruitment. Group management told it to cancel it – even if it got the new sales people on board now, it was a nine-month sales cycle and they wouldn't have time to sell anything in the current financial year. Current year's profitability was saved. The 'long run' in this case was six months. In the budget meeting the following autumn, the company had a hard time about the low sales growth it was projecting for the next year. You remember the sales people you told us not to recruit six months ago? They were the ones who were going to produce the growth.

Action Points on the Future

○ *Be honest* with yourself (and I mean really, really honest) about what spending supports current activity and what creates the future.

○ *Be realistic* about the tradeoffs between today and tomorrow – recognise that short-term performance does to some extent come at the cost of long-term growth and development. Look for the best tradeoffs, rather than trying to pretend that they don't exist.

○ *Make sure you are clear* – in the management team, among the stakeholders – about the balance between short-term performance and long-term prosperity. Be prepared for some tricky discussions, as this is a question of values, not logic. It's about what you want, not the best way of getting it. You may need to adjust the balance more towards the short term, but unless you are in real crisis (that is to say, facing a real threat to your corporate survival), don't neglect the future.

The Wrong Market

This issue could also be called, rather cruelly, 'customers don't care'. There's nothing inherently wrong with your product, it's just that the market doesn't value it.

Take an example from the airline industry. I write this on a cold and wet February day, so I thought I'd cheer myself up by starting to plan my summer holiday. I am thinking of Tuscany, so looked up flights to and from Pisa for the first two weeks of August. It turns out that there are three options for direct flights: Ryanair from Stansted, Easyjet from Luton and British Airways from Gatwick.

Choosing the flights at civilised times, these were the prices:

Ryanair – £150
Easyjet – £147
British Airways – £207

Which would I choose? If I am travelling on business (that is, on someone else's money), I'll always chose BA over Ryanair or Easyjet. It is a more pleasant experience. On holiday, however, I'm inclined to go for the cheapest – we're a family of five and the saving is attractive.

You have to wonder why BA is flying to Pisa at all. Tuscany isn't exactly a major commercial centre at any time, and in August any business that isn't tourist-related is closed.

Although BA is charging higher fares, I suspect that while Ryanair and Easyjet are making money on this route, BA isn't. Their roots are in that distant age when air travel was a glamorous luxury, and some of the legacy remains – for example, as noted previously, BA's most senior cabin crew earn twice as much as Ryanair or Easyjet pay theirs.

The bottom line for BA is this: you are set up to provide

a superior experience, something that at least one business traveller (me) cares enough about to pay something extra for (unless his clients really, really insist). You need to be operating routes on which there are decent numbers of business travellers, not ones dominated by holidaymakers who just want the lowest price. New York, definitely. Milan, very probably. Pisa, unlikely.

The airline example is an obvious one – obvious enough for me to be able to dissect it from the outside. Sometimes, however, the same phenomenon – customers who care in one context and don't care in another – can be harder to spot, and you might need to do some work to uncover it. A marketing consultancy did this, and received a startling new insight.

The core business was helping pharmaceutical companies use their clinical data to develop marketing messages. They had masses of data from clinical trials, which they used to get new products approved. The consultancy's job was to analyse the data and see what marketing uses it could be put to. Was there evidence that made it the drug of choice for patients with kidney problems? Or perhaps it could demonstrate that while it was no better than its competitors' products in adults, it had fewer side-effects in the over-75s?

If the consultancy could do this, it was enormously valuable to its clients. They were launching new drugs in which they had invested hundreds of millions of pounds. The market was usually competitive, so the difference between launching the product well and launching it badly amounted to hundreds of millions of pounds over its life.

The other reason the consultancy was valuable was that only it could do this. You needed to understand both science and marketing. It employed people with PhDs in subjects like biochemistry, who also understood pharmaceutical marketing. Nobody in the pharmaceutical companies had this mix of knowledge. Of course they employed thousands of scientists of all disciplines, but they didn't get the marketing side. The marketing people didn't have the scientific background. The consultancy was in a unique position, so why was it struggling to make money?

The answer turned out to be that it was in two markets, not one. Looking at the profitability of all the projects done over the past three years, there were some very large differences. Sometimes it was 'scientific' work – analysing data, and helping clients communicate it to the international community of doctors whose endorsement (or lack of endorsement) would greatly influence the product's success. Other times, it was 'marketing' work, like support material for pharmaceutical reps to use when visiting ordinary doctors. Superficially these different types of work looked the same, but there was a *fundamental difference in the client's frame of mind, and therefore their willingness to pay.*

For the scientific work, the client was thinking: 'How on earth can I deal with all this data that I can't understand? Thank goodness you're here.' They were lost, and the consultancy was rescuing them. For the marketing stuff, on the other hand, the clients felt on firmer ground. It was something like: 'I could do this myself, but I don't have the time. I can outsource it to some clowns.' It was often the same people in both cases, but in different frames of mind.

The bottom line is this: if you are anything but the rock-bottom, lowest cost, cheapest and most cheerful player in the market, there are customers out there who just don't care about the superiority of your offering and won't pay extra for it. Don't take it personally, but don't try to sell to these folks.

Action Points on Customers

Be sure everyone is in agreement on the answers to two questions:

 What do we offer?

❷ Who cares?

The answer to the first could be:

- *Superior quality* – not high quality, everyone offers that; I mean superior to others in a quantifiable way
- *Superior service*
- *Faster delivery*
- *Lower prices*

The second question means: who cares enough about our point of difference to pay extra for it, or choose us rather than the competition?

If the product doesn't match the market, we have broken Mike's ROI rule – we are spending money on being superior in a way that doesn't produce a return in the form of higher sales or higher prices.

The Wrong Products

Very often, I find companies selling products which actually cost them money. There is a whole range of reasons why products can be unprofitable. The reasons may vary, but the bottom line is the same: sometimes products are just inherently unprofitable and cutting costs isn't going to solve the problem. The way to solve the problem is to find the offending products and either fix them or eliminate them. I have found this to be a very powerful way of raising profitability, and I'm not alone. I was speaking recently to someone who runs a large private equity portfolio, who told me that it was a centrepiece of their approach as well.

Given that your product portfolio may be infested with loss-makers, how do you track them down and root them out? Here are some of the reasons, and the clues you can look for to identify the culprits.

They are commodities. The same thing, or something very like the same thing, is available from many different suppliers. Customers don't care about the differences between suppliers, and just go for the cheapest. In this case, only one supplier may be making money. In some cases, nobody may be making money. How can you spot whether your product portfolio contains some of these? An honest talk with the sales force is probably all it takes. Which are the lines that are available easily from your competitors? Which are the lines where the customers make decisions solely on price? Unless you are sure, very sure, that you have the lowest costs in the industry, you have at least grounds for suspicion that you are losing money on these lines.

They have never been properly costed. Seems weird, but it happens all the time. Notoriously, the original Mini, launched in 1959, was a hugely successful car, but made no money at all for the then British Motor Corporation. The costs hadn't been properly calculated, and it was sold for too little. One of my clients, a logistics company in Belgium, had been through a period of setting contract prices on the basis of little more than gut feeling. It wasn't then completely surprising when they did a proper profitability study and found one contract costing them 20% of turnover. If some of your products need customisation, and you don't have a proper job-costing system, then some of them are probably costing you money. If lots of different things go through the same production process and you don't have a good way of allocating the cost of the process, some of what comes out is probably unprofitable.

They are what Peter Drucker calls 'unjustified special-ities'. They have complications that other products don't, which makes them more expensive to manufacture but no more valuable to the customer. So the customer won't buy at a price that covers costs.

Action Points on Products

Become a products detective. Your working assumption is that some things in the product portfolio are costing you money. Your task is to find them and deal with them. Use the clues above to *cut through detailed analysis and take action.*

Another Really Bad Way to Cut Costs

Imagine this: 'To plan our headcount reduction, we are going to write all the employees' names on the wall. Then I'll close my eyes and throw darts. The ones who get hit leave the company. The process will be just about random, but we'll tweak it slightly by writing the better employees' names larger so that they're more likely to be taken out.'

Yes, it sounds demented. But it goes on all the time. It's called a recruitment freeze. Stop hiring and wait for people to leave, until you have painlessly (!) reduced numbers. It's not hard to see the problems. The process is random. You've decided that you need to do more marketing and less sales, but if a first-class marketing person hands in their notice and a mediocre sales person doesn't, then you reduce marketing. The bias towards canning the better people happens because, once your staff realise what you're doing, the depths of desperation and stupidity you've descended to, they quite sensibly decide to leave. The faster they catch on, and the better their prospects elsewhere, the sooner they're off. As a way of lowering the average quality of the workforce, the recruitment freeze is hard to beat.

The freeze is popular because the alternative takes guts. To be making some people redundant while still recruiting others takes strength of character and clarity of intention. You need to do some very hard thinking and take some agonising decisions about who's essential and who's not, while dealing with those who have to leave is no fun. In hard times, the right thing is neither the easy thing nor the popular thing.

Action Point on Recruitment Freezes
Don't.

You're Too Small

The business, that is, not you personally. This is quite a common issue, and one which won't respond to cost reduction. You need, gulp, 'a strategic solution', which is to say a long hard think about the shape of the business.

Very often, what we find in this case is a version of the 'stuck in the middle' syndrome. You could be successful if you were 50% or more smaller, as a specialist or niche player, or you could be successful if you were quite a lot larger, but you can't be successful at the size you are.

The marketing consultancy mentioned earlier came across a very painful version of this issue. It worked out the number of different specialisms needed in the company to provide the level of service the clients expected – scientific writing, print production, meeting planning and organisation, PR ... Each of these functions needed a small pyramid of senior, middle-level and junior people, otherwise costs were too high and the senior people got fed up doing low-level work. The result of this thought process was that the company needed about 45 people. It had 30, and just enough business to keep them occupied. To satisfy stakeholders' expectations, the company needed to grow by 50%, very fast.

That would have worked, if they could have got there. Alternatively, the company could have headed in the opposite direction, becoming more specialised. It could just have done strategic advice and not the execution part of it in the form of printed materials and meetings. Or it could have become more 'plain vanilla', with more emphasis on getting stuff done rather than advising. Or.... There were lots of possibilities, but one thing that didn't work was the status quo.

I ran across the same issue more recently, when I was helping a manufacturer of industrial components. They had a warehouse in Spain, and their value to most customers was that they probably had the part you wanted in stock, and could get it to you the next day. In fact, you could drive over to the warehouse yourself and pick it up if you wanted. Unfortunately, a warehouse is a fixed cost, and this company needed about 25% more sales to cover it. The alternatives were either to shrink, close the warehouse and serve only those few major customers who were already being supplied from the group's factories elsewhere in Europe, or grow the business to the point where it covered the fixed cost. They chose the second route, with an investment in sales management to ensure that the growth happened.

Action Points on Getting to the Right Size

Don't be misled by those mealy-mouthed managers and consultants who have made 'right-sizing' a euphemism for cutting back. *Recognise that getting to the right size might mean growing.* Getting smaller doesn't mean doing a bit less of everything, either. It's not about becoming a smaller elephant; it's more like transforming from an elephant into a monkey.

Once you start looking at ways to change the shape of the business, you need to start joining things up. Make sure you have done the work on product profitability and customers. If you want to shrink the business, make sure you move the emphasis towards those who make the best profits. If your conclusion is that you need to grow, be sure to be clear about which types of customer and product produce the growth, because you obviously want to be sure that growth is profitable. This is called 'integrating strategy and finance', and is often done very badly. Do it even reasonably well, and you will be safely in the top quartile.

PUTTING IT ALL TOGETHER

There's a logical order to work through all of this. Doing it in the right order saves you from being overwhelmed. You also might get lucky – if you identify the problem at step one or step two, you won't need to do the subsequent steps.

Step 1 – eliminate waste and surplus capacity. This is a no-brainer. Just make sure you remember the ROI rule, and apply it to the time you spend. Don't spend days of your valuable time trying to get the last few thousand pounds out.

Step 2 – clarify your thoughts about how much you value the long term versus the short term. How much long-term potential are you willing to sacrifice for short-term results? Be very sure that you have thrashed this out very thoroughly. If you try to finesse the issue at this stage, disagreements will keep resurfacing to trip you up and slow you down at every step of the way. You will also sow confusion, mistrust and demoralisation. Set the level of investment spending where you want it to be.

Step 3 – make sure your pricing is up to scratch. Until you've done this, you don't know the potential of the business.

Step 4 – understand products and customers. Making use of this information will boost profits, and you need it for the next step.

If you have reached this point and solved your problem, congratulations. If not, you need to move on to the next and scariest step:

Step 5 – strategic review. The business is the wrong shape. You need to fix this, but at least you now have the information you need.

CHAPTER 4

MEASUREMENT

YOU CAN MEASURE IT, BUT SHOULD YOU MANAGE IT?

Here is the state of measurement in most organisations:

▶ We know what's happened, but we don't know why.
▶ We don't know what to do to improve results.

This is because:

▶ We are mostly measuring the wrong things.

That is the state of things if you are lucky. It's quite possible that some of the things we do measure, and therefore try to manage, pull us in completely the wrong direction. It's also possible that the finance department, i.e., the people you need to help you in this area, are in fact part of the problem.

In short, it's a mess. The good news, however, is that it is one of the easier problems in business to solve. The principles are simple, and the maths required is no more than arithmetic. It's a simply a matter of applying a little logic to accounting conventions and making sure that, for once, the logic wins.

GROSS PROFIT MARGIN: GROSSLY MISLEADING

When I worked in a marketing consultancy, the question of gross margin caused me a lot of head-scratching. The company had evolved from a publishing house, so gross margin was a key measure. It was defined in a completely standard way, as revenue less costs of print, typesetting, freelance editorial, illustration, etc. Basically, revenue less external cost. Margins were very variable. Some projects, like the strategic publishing programme, had a gross margin close to 100%. The strategic publishing programme was a consultancy offering, where our highly qualified staff put their heads together and developed a marketing strategy for the client. The staff costs were recorded as overhead, so accordingly we had an impressively high gross margin.

At the other end of the gross margin scale came the book reprinting programme, where we only made a gross margin of 20–25%. The conclusion seemed pretty clear – strategic publishing programmes, with lots of senior-level staff input = good, reprints = bad.

There was however a problem. Although the company was enjoying very attractive gross margins, it was struggling to make money. In fact, it was struggling to get the work out of the door. This was because judging projects on the basis of their gross margin missed the most important point about the company. It used highly specialised staff, who were expensive to employ and hard to find.

The crucial question for us was which sorts of products or services made the best use of our scarce and expensive staff. The 'attractive' product with the high gross margins was extremely labour-intensive. Adopting a measure based on this idea changed the picture completely. The measure was very simple: how much did we make for each hour of staff time spent on a project? Looked at in this way, the order of merit was reversed. The labour-intensive strategic publishing programme turned out to be one of the lowest-value activities, as it soaked up so much senior-level time. It might, if it went well, make £100 per hour. The humble reprint, on the other hand, turned out to be a star. The low gross margin was more than compensated for by the fact that we didn't really have to do anything to complete the project. One fax to the printer asking for quotes for different quantities, one fax to the client with a quotation, followed by a fax to the printer confirming quantities and delivery address, and the job was done. Easily £1,000 per hour – so how could this be bad business? Yet our old financial reporting, which focused on gross margin, made it so.

Without this insight, we could have ended up in a horrible mess. We would have charged ahead and sold lots of strategic publishing programmes. Our forecast gross margin would have been fantastic, but then we would have hit a problem. Either we just wouldn't have been able to deliver the work, or we would have needed to take on so many extra people that we lost money.

Focusing on gross margin can prevent you from understanding how your business works, and what sorts of products or services are best for it. In fact it can do even worse than that – it can prevent you from doing sensible things. Take this example from Starbucks. (Please don't tell me that you can get a better cup of coffee somewhere else – I don't care. From a commercial point of view, these guys are brilliant.)

While waiting for a cup of coffee one day in Starbucks, I passed the time by analysing their gross margin. I noticed something very interesting.

Here are the approximate economics of a tall latte, in pence. I have costed the ingredients at supermarket prices, which will be close enough.

Price to customer	210
Cost of half a pint of milk	35
Cost of 7g of coffee	7
Gross profit	168
Gross profit percentage	80%

There is an option to have a stronger coffee, by adding an extra shot of espresso to the same size cup. See what happens if you order the extra shot:

Price of extra shot to customer	15
Cost of extra 7g of coffee	7
Gross profit of extra shot on its own	8
Gross profit percentage of extra shot on its own	53%
Combined gross profit percentage of coffee plus extra shot	78%

So offering the extra shot has actually *reduced* the gross profit percentage! And yet it is a good idea. Here is the logic.

Most of your costs in a coffee shop are fixed – they relate to the costs of staff, and the costs of retail space. The number of people you can get in the door is, in the short term, fixed. It depends on where you are, how many people are passing and how many other coffee shops there are in the neighbourhood. One way to boost profit is to sell more to the customers who do come in. This is what the extra shot does. It takes no extra work, and does not change the cost of staff or space. It gives an extra free 8p for every customer who asks for it.

If Starbucks thought in terms of gross margin they would either not offer the extra shot, or offer it at a price which kept the gross profit percentage at 80%. That would be 35p, at which point it starts to look too expensive for all but the really, really hardcore caffeine addicts. Either approach would have the same effect – raising the gross profit percentage reduces the profit. What the extra shot does is to lower the profit per pound of sales, but raise the profit per customer, and hence the profit per location.

Gross profit percentage, in both these examples, produces a misleading result. The reason is the same in both cases. Both the marketing consultancy and the coffee shop have a 'limiting factor', i.e., a constraint on the level of business they can do. For the marketing consultancy, it is the number of qualified staff it can recruit. For the coffee shop, it is the number of customers who walk in the door. For both businesses, the right measure is one based on the limiting factor. For the marketing consultancy, that is profit per hour. For Starbucks, it is profit per visit.

Note that the useful measures have two things in common:

- ◉ They are not revenue related to revenue (like gross profit as percentage of sales) but revenue related to something that isn't money (profit per hour, or per customer).
- ◉ They are very specific to the particular business and its individual circumstances.

We will come back to these points later in the chapter.

WHY NET MARGIN IS NOT A USEFUL MEASURE

16.7%. Even after 15 years, the figure is etched on my mind. This was, according to an analyst's report, the average operating profit margin for business and professional publishing. At the time, I was Commercial Director of a subsidiary of a large business and professional publishing group, whose margin was 9%. The group management had been told that this had to rise to 12% pretty quickly, or they would be history.

My company was something of an oddball within the

group. It wasn't really a publishing company, but a consultancy. Looking at its immediate peer group, I saw that they achieved margins of 10% in a good year. How were we going to reach 16.7%? Some of what we did made sense. We developed a really good understanding of which projects made money and which didn't. We developed much better metrics to tell us how we were doing and what to do more of. And we shared information much more widely, and educated financially far more of our staff than any other company I have seen before or since.

Unfortunately, we also had to do some rather less constructive things:

● We restricted growth in the short term.
● We increased the level of risk in the business to alarming and unnecessary levels.

But worst of all:

● We completely missed the future.

The financial story of this business illustrates the horrors which can lurk behind a healthy-seeming profit margin. We restricted growth by cutting back on the expenditure needed to produce growth. This reached its peak one March, when we were reviewing plans based on first-quarter results. Sales weren't developing as well as we had forecast. We had planned to recruit an extra sales person, but hadn't yet done so. The parent company saw an opportunity to contain costs. In our business it took at least nine months for new sales people to produce revenue, so the planned new person was going to have a negative effect on the current year. Cancel the recruitment, we were told, and save the money. You won't lose any sales this year. That is what we did. Was it surprising, six months later when doing next year's budget, that we were struggling to find growth?

This highlights a big problem with conventional management accounts. They treat costs as costs, whether they produce benefits in the present or in the future. The costs of sales activity and customer service that support this year's sales are treated indistinguishably from the costs of marketing and product development that support future years. Add to this the fact that management accounts force you to ignore anything that might happen after the end of the current accounting year (even if that is only three months ahead) and it is easy to see how investment can be stifled.

We increased the risk in the business by taking out safety margins. Our plan didn't, couldn't, include much of an allowance for problem projects, new staff not performing as well or as quickly as planned, client losses or any of the other routine risks of business. This made everything very fragile.

Finally, and probably worst of all, we missed the future. Behind the daily round of frantic activity, a profound change was going on. Historically, we had helped our clients, major pharmaceutical companies, market their products by developing messages about clinical efficacy aimed at doctors, i.e., the ones who made the prescribing decisions. In many cases, the doctor writing the prescription didn't actually know how much the product cost. This was changing. In a bid to contain costs, more and more healthcare providers were beginning to look at cost-effectiveness. If a product wasn't judged cost-effective, the doctor could not prescribe it, no matter what he or she thought about its efficacy. The industry needed to start developing messages for economists, about cost-effectiveness, if it wanted to maintain sales. We 'sort of' recognised this, but didn't do anything about it – we simply didn't have time, being so stretched to keep the current business running. Over a few years the economists increased their power over the doctors, and we had nothing to say to them to promote our clients' products. Our ability to communicate with the doctors became less and less valuable.

THE PROFIT–GROWTH–RISK TRIANGLE

When it comes to net margin, the reality is like the old saying, 'Good, cheap, fast. Choose any two.' You can have a good job done fast, but it won't be cheap. Or you can have a cheap job done fast, but it won't be good.

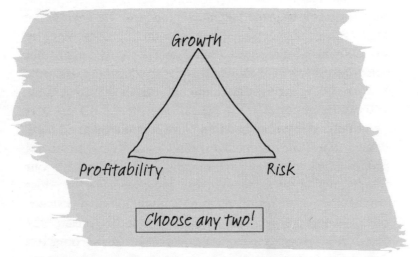

In this case, the three corners of the triangle are growth, risk and profitability, and the most interesting of the three is risk. Many people recognise, at least in principle, that growth usually requires some short-term sacrifice of profitability, but the role of risk is less overt. Often, it tends to be 'secret sauce', the hidden ingredient which enhances flavour without extra cost. Unfortunately, like the excess monosodium glutamate in a questionable oriental meal, it leaves a nasty aftertaste.

One of the most egregious examples of the misuse of risk is illustrated by the case of the BP Texas City refinery. In 2005 an explosion there killed 15 people and injured 170.

The refinery management had previously been ordered to reduce costs by 25%, and a report by the US Government Chemical Safety Board concluded that this had been a significant factor in the disaster. Planned and preventative maintenance had been cut back, and worn out plant not replaced.

It's unlikely that anything you do in your business would have the same consequences as a major refinery explosion, but ignoring any corner of the triangle can still lead you to disaster.

So the answer is to stop kidding yourself. If you decide that you want to grow faster, assume that you need either to increase cost (and hence sacrifice profitability) or increase risk, unless you have very good reasons for thinking otherwise. Companies like Toyota do manage to keep lowering costs at the same time as they raise quality, without (usually) increasing risk, but that is because they work on it every day, and they have a method for doing it. What's more, they don't work directly on cost, but on the process which underlies both cost and quality. It's one thing to ask, 'How do we improve our processes to reduce costs?' and invent a process for improving your processes. It is something else to ask, 'How do we reduce costs?' The first can produce genuine improvements; the second, if it does reduce costs, will probably do so only at the expense of increasing risk.

To grow, you will need to actively manage risk. Everyone accepts this. It is less usual to recognise that cutting costs also requires risk management. You will need a clever plan. Think of what would have happened if the Texas City refinery had been asked to increase its capacity by 25% rather than reducing costs by the same percentage. This would have been a major capital project with a heavyweight project team, steering committee, risk management plan, the full works. It would probably have been done very well. But where was the risk management for a major cost reduction? It just wasn't there.

WHAT MANAGEMENT ACCOUNTS DON'T TELL YOU

It would be quicker to say what management accounts do tell. It is this: 'In total, things are/are not developing in accordance with plan.'

That's all. Useful, I suppose, but wouldn't you also want to know:

- ○ Whether in detail things are developing in line with plan, or whether they are developing quite differently, and that it's just a coincidence the totals come out the same.
- ○ Whether things will continue to develop in line with plan.
- ○ Whether the plan was realistic in the first place.
- ○ And finally, the most important question of all: What do we do to improve results?

All this is possible. It is not even particularly hard, but you will need to go beyond management accounts to get it.

Take a couple of examples. Suppose, for instance, that the management accounts tell us that sales are up. Why? Is this healthy trend likely to continue? What can we do to make things even better?

There are three reasons why sales could be up:

- ○ We have more customers.
- ○ We have the same number of customers, or fewer, but they are buying more from us each time.
- ○ We have the same number of customers, they buy the same each time, but they buy more often.

These three different reasons lead us to completely different conclusions, and suggest three different courses of action. The plan for acquiring more customers is quite different from the plan for selling more to existing customers, or persuading existing customers to buy more often. It would be hard to find anything which is less like rocket science, but standard management accounts don't give us this information.

We don't know what is driving the results so we don't know what to do to make them improve, and even if we make a guess at the best course of action we aren't told whether it is having the desired result. For instance, suppose we decide to make a real effort to grow sales by increasing the average value of the sale – i.e., selling more to each customer each time they buy. We do that, and sales rise. But how do we know that sales rose because of our efforts to increase the size of each sale? Maybe our efforts in this area achieved negligible results, and the improvement comes from new customers, or from customers buying more often.

Management accounts can obscure truly terrifying trends. A good example of management account illusion comes from the academic journal industry, which went through a near-death experience in the 1990s. In the 1980s, publishers of scientific journals realised that they had the closest legal equivalent to a monopoly on the supply of crack cocaine. A scientific paper published in a journal was in essence a small monopoly – available only to subscribers in that journal. An important paper was considered essential. The addictive quality came from the fact that librarians hated 'broken series'. Once they had started subscribing to a periodical, they hated to stop.

The publishers took full advantage of their mono-polistic power over this highly addictive product, with swingeing price increases. Pierre Vinken, chairman of the major publisher Elsevier, put it very succinctly: 'Our model is very simple – you put up the prices and take in the money.' The good times rolled... but... Behind a very healthy upward trend in revenue and profit was a worrying reality. Every year, as prices rose, subscriber numbers fell. Extrapolate the trend, and you arrived at a point where each journal would have one subscriber, paying a six- or seven-figure sum. This was clearly not sustainable. By the mid-1990s there was a real sense of crisis in the industry, with real anger towards the publishers on the part of their customers and an attempt by academics (the publishers' customers) to use new technology to destroy the existing system, and hence the existing publishers. Having your customers hating you and working to undermine your business model is rarely good for business, yet all through this time, the management accounts said everything was going very nicely.

EFFICIENCY MEASURES DESTROY EFFICIENCY

It would seem to make good sense to go beyond management accounts, and produce other measures to manage performance. Well, yes, but often no.

The sad fact is, it's not difficult to come up with efficiency measures which actively work to *lower* performance.

The following story is in the public domain, but it is typical of many.

In June 2005, prominent journalist Jeff Jarvis posted this on his blog (http://www.buzzmachine.com/), under the title 'Dell Lies, Dell Sucks':

> *I just got a new Dell laptop and paid a fortune for the four-year, in-home service. The machine is a lemon and the service is a lie. I'm having all kinds of trouble with the hardware: overheats, network doesn't work, maxes out on CPU usage. It's a lemon.*

In a subsequent article that appeared on the *Guardian* website (August 2005), Jarvis described the way the issue exploded all over the web:

It snowballed into a saga, a weblog miniseries. Scores of readers left comments with their stories of Dell hell and scores more bloggers linked to my post with their wails of woe. I updated my audience with my latest tales of transoceanic frustration: I'd paid for home service but couldn't get it; Dell replaced half my machine but it still wouldn't work . . . I can't take credit or blame for this, but in the midst of this silicon opera, Dell's customer satisfaction rating, market share, and share price in the US all shrank.

Serious stuff. There has been a lot of comment about this saga, mostly focused on the importance of listening to customers. Dell now employs people to monitor the blogosphere and respond to complaints. The other side of the story, the one I want to look at here, is how Dell came to be offering such poor service in the first place. It all stems from a mistaken idea of how to measure efficiency.

Dell had been tracking 'handle time' per call, but this just encouraged operators to transfer callers, simply making them someone else's problem. Some 45% of calls were being transferred, with 7,000 of the 400,000 customers calling each week being transferred seven times or more.

At about the same time I also had problems with Dell, in the course of which they sent an engineer out five times to change different parts. It didn't help my computer, which didn't surprise me as it seemed to me that I had a software problem. It did, however, help the Dell operator, offering them a quick way of ending the call. The net financial effect on Dell, even ignoring the damage to customer goodwill and reputation, was horribly negative. I don't know what a futile engineer visit cost, but it must be the equivalent of several hours' phone time. By the time they had sent the engineer five times, they would have done better just to have given me a new machine. The whole saga was ruinously expensive for Dell, but according to the 'handle time' measure, everything was going fine – the calls were short, because each time I called they fobbed me off with another engineer visit.

Dell had created a system which positively encouraged and rewarded poor service. The faster an operator got the customer off the phone (with an offer of a non-solution like a visit from an engineer) or transferred them elsewhere, the more frustrated the customer became and *the better the metrics looked*.

The answer for Dell, in retrospect, was really simple. Stop focusing on the handle time of an individual call, and instead start measuring the minutes per resolution of a problem, regardless of how many calls it took. Aim to resolve as many problems as possible in one call, no matter how long the call is.

There are many examples of how using a simple-minded measure produces dysfunctional results. Here are just a few:

❶ Hospitals set a target of 'nobody has to wait longer than x weeks for treatment' start prioritising less urgent cases who are close to the time limit rather than more urgent cases who joined the waiting list later.

❷ Sales staff set targets for revenue meet those targets by 'buying the business' – i.e. giving it away at ridiculously high discounts which lose money for the company.

❸ Teachers assessed strictly on exam results concentrate on 'teaching to the test', resulting in boring lessons and turning the pupils away from following the subject to a higher level.

SENSIBLE MEASUREMENT – IT DOES EXIST

Dell had to drag their former head of manufacturing out of retirement to solve their problem. But it shouldn't be so hard. Here are some principles to help you do it yourself:

First of all, *make sure you aren't being lazy*. It's tempting to focus on a few simple measures, or just one even simpler measure, but most of the time that would be a bad idea. Rembember the maxim 'things should be made as simple as possible, but no simpler.' If the situation is complex, you cannot avoid that complexity. You have to deal with it.

Focus on the whole process. For example, if you are doing anything in the area of sales, you need to look at the whole sales process from negotiation through processing of the order, shipping the item or scheduling the person to perform the task, to invoicing, collecting the cash and providing any after-sales service. The reason for this is that it is so easy for people running part of the process to optimise their part of it in ways that create problems further down the line. For instance, sales people can make sales by making unrealistic promises about what the product will do or how easy it will be to use. This will create extra costs in customer service. Whether your measure is cost, speed or quality, it has to be based on the whole process, not a part of it.

Measure something that matters to the customer. In the case of Dell, I don't think many customers cared how long an individual call was. Dell thought this was important, because they wanted to keep costs down. The customers, on the other hand, cared about how long it took from having a problem to having it resolved. Get the process working right first – low error rates, high rate of 'getting it right first time' – and you will probably find that the costs come down as well. Getting it right first time is usually very cost-effective.

Assume that people will try to game the system. If you tell people 'these are the measures on which you are judged' then they quite reasonably will do their best to score as highly as possible on those measures even if they see that doing so doesn't produce the best result for the customer or the company. Ask yourself whether there is any way in which you could hit the measures and yet not produce best possible results and profitability. If it's possible, assume it will happen.

YOU DON'T NEED A FINANCE DIRECTOR, YOU NEED TWO FINANCE DIRECTORS

Measurement seems to be a horrible mess in so many companies. We don't know how we're doing against the key variables, we don't know what to do to improve things, and often the measures we do have are actually driving us to make things worse. Given that so much of this measurement comes (or should be coming) from the finance department, hadn't we better ask what the Finance Director is doing?

This is not intended as an attack on finance people. I was an FD myself for years, and still think that they do a vital job, and usually do it well. The problem is, the vital job that they usually do well is only one of the two vital jobs they need to do. Worse, *the very things that make them good at the first vital job make it very difficult for them to do the other vital job.*

To explain, you need first to understand what the two jobs are. Then see why the skills, attributes and mindsets that lead to success in one are positively unhelpful in the other. The two jobs are:

❶ *Head of control and compliance.* Produce the basic accounts. Make sure customers pay when they should. Prevent people spending money they shouldn't be spending, or stealing from the company. Make sure the bills get paid on time, that the tax returns are done and the tax is paid when it should be.

❷ *Business partner.* Start each day thinking, 'How can I help this organisation to make more money?'

For the first job, control and compliance, a number of principles are important:

- *Consistency.* The whole point of published accounts is to allow shareholders, who may not know much about the company, to compare its results with those of others. The format has to be standardised, and transactions treated the same way year on year. It's no good at all counting salaries of marketing staff as part of 'marketing costs' one year and 'salaries' the next, or reporting sales by product type one year and customer type the next.
- *Regularity.* You have to commit to regular accounting periods. The ruling party in the British parliament can call a general election at whatever time it thinks most propitious for re-election, but a company can't decide to have a year end at whatever time produces the best results.
- *Low level of detail.* Sets of accounts need to be a manageable size, which means that they can't go into huge levels of detail.
- *High level of accuracy.* Accounts need to be pretty near right. You can't publish a statement saying, 'Last year's profit was £5m, give or take a million.' If you are saying it is £5m, it had better be between £4.9m and £5.1m.

Now here is the shocker. See how these principles, right and proper for the first job, actually get in the way of the second task of being a business partner.

Consistency is a bad thing. In fact, you need to be completely inconsistent. One day you are interested in how the product range is developing. Which products are growing, which are declining? So you do all your analysis by product. Next month you are interested in customers: what type of customer is most profitable? So you redo everything by customer.

Regularity has little value to the business partner. Times change, and different issues come to the fore. Some things change very quickly, and may need to be looked at daily or weekly. Some things change slowly and may only merit a look every few years.

Detail is crucial. Much of the work of the business partner is based on picking apart the aggregated numbers in the accounts, in a way that produces insight. You need to dig down, but selectively. It's a question of minute analysis of some areas and complete disregard of others.

Level of accuracy has to vary according to the task, but usually it is less than for the formal accounts. A certain type of customer may be twice as proftable as the norm, or six times. It doesn't matter, because the conclusion in either case is the same – we want more like this.

SO WHAT IS A GOOD MEASUREMENT?

This chapter isn't arguing against the value of measurement. It's arguing against stupid counterproductive measurement, in favour of useful measurement. Here are some of the principles to look out for.

Measurement is useful when it is tailored to the particular business, and that business's particular issues at a particular time. For the marketing consultancy, the issue was the limit on staff numbers. For Starbucks, it was the need to maximise income per customer. Go back to those organisations a few years later, and you might well find that the issues have changed. If so, the reporting needs to change as well.

Measures involving revenue related to revenue (gross profit to sales, for example) tend to be much less useful than measures relating revenue to something else. For example, these can be extremely useful:

● *Costs of whole processes, not parts.* For instance, knowing the cost of entering a sales order is much less useful than knowing the cost of the sales order process in its entirety – from entering the order through picking and despatch to invoicing and cash collection. Looking at the cost of a whole process avoids the danger of sub-optimisation, where one department optimises its own operations by imposing costs on others.

● *Cost of serving a customer*, including cost of selling to them.

● *Lifetime value of a customer.* This is a very good measure. Not only does it relate revenue to customers, but it also transcends accounting years.

● *Cost of acquiring a new customer.* Tracking this over time gives a good leading indicator of the future health of the business. If the cost of gaining new customers is rising then something is happening in the market that will have consequences later. You need to start preparing now. Relating the cost of acquiring a new customer to the lifetime value of a customer will tell you whether your business is sustainable in the long term.

Useful measurement is usually available at a much more detailed level than conventional management accounts. Reporting sales by five or six product types is much less useful than analysing it by individual customer, product or sales channel.

Because useful information needs to be based on very detailed analysis, it has to include more commentary, that is to say, more words and fewer numbers. You can't circulate a report showing the profitability of each of your 3,000 customers. You can – in fact should – circulate a report saying something like 'Customers doing less than £50,000 of business a year are generally at best marginally profitable. Those doing over £250,000 are generally good, but with these few exceptions which we need to investigate.'

There's a lot of social conformity involved here, and that is likely to be the biggest obstacle to overcome in bringing some sense to the question of measurement. There are strong beliefs about the 'proper' things to measure, and some of those will be wrong for your organisation.

On the other hand, good measurement can make a huge difference in understanding the true causes of things, and in pointing the way to improvement. Changing what you measure can have a real impact on what, and how, you do things.

CHAPTER 5

BUDGETING AND PLANNING

Imagine what it would be like if you ran your life according to the principles of corporate budgeting.

You would like to get a new job, and you know you are well qualified. You could increase your salary substantially, and enjoy work much more. You have a two-month window in the year, from September to October, in which you will entertain job offers. If a headhunter calls during the other ten months, you ignore them.

Your daughter is moving school this year. The nearest one, which she's sure to get into, is perfectly fine. However, there is another one a little further away which is truly exceptional. Her chances of getting into this one are about 50%. You don't apply, because if your daughter doesn't get in, your wife will kill you. In fact, you do your best to conceal from both wife and daughter the fact that there is any chance of getting into this fabulous school.

You want to move house. In September you need to decide where you are going to move to, and how much it will cost. If the plan changes, because you can't find anything you like at the price you decided or you decide you prefer another area, you can't change the plan, even if you can afford the extra money.

In November you realise that you haven't had to spend anything on car repairs. You had expected to spend £500, so you have the car serviced again, twice.

A friend offers you the use of their holiday home in France for a week in May. You have the time and you would like to go. The only cost to you is the cost of getting there, which is no problem at all – it's less than the amount you saved on car repairs. However, since you have no allowance for travel costs, you say no.

In October you are offered a lucrative piece of free-lance work. The client wants it done as soon as possible, and you could do it in a couple of weeks. You try to persuade them to wait until January, because you have already earned as much as you planned to this calendar year.

And so on . . .

Now I don't for a moment suppose that you do run your life like this. If you did, you wouldn't be reading this book, since nobody budgets for books telling them that everything they know is wrong. And yet, in the corporate world, this bizarre behaviour is the norm.

HOW BUDGETS KILL OPPORTUNITIES

This is a true story, told to me by the man himself.

Mark was a partner in a firm of accountants. He developed a piece of tax planning software for his own use, then realised it could be sold to other firms as well. He paid £1,000 for an advertisement on the back page of *Accountancy* magazine, and did very well. He sold £6,000 of software in a month. Reasonably enough, he thought it was worth doing again. He went to his partners in the firm and asked to spend another £1,000 on advertising. What did they think? Maybe they wouldn't sell £6,000 this time, but they would certainly make money. It looked like the classic 'no-brainer' proposal. It did in fact get a no-brain response, but not the one Mark was expecting: '*We can't do that, we've spent the marketing budget for the year.*'

These are the sorts of people who just wouldn't listen to someone offering them a new job, if they didn't call in

September or October. I am sure that in their private lives they weren't that stupid, but there seems to be something about the budgeting process which leads a great many people to leave their common sense at the door when they come to work.

What Mark's colleagues are in fact saying is this. 'Once a year, in September or October, we will sit down and decide what is going to happen up to the end of the next financial year, that is, fifteen months hence. Any opportunities need to be visible now, or we are going to ignore them. If something comes up later we won't take advantage of it.' Notice that Mark's proposal isn't asking them to sacrifice any profit this year in favour of future years. The great thing about placing an advert for software is that it makes money in the same year. In fact, it probably goes into profit within a month. If you're really clever, you can have the customers pay by cheque or credit card and have their money in the bank before you pay *Accountancy* magazine for the advertising space. All good for your cashflow.

The unusual thing about this story is not the bone-headed response. That is unfortunately common. What is unusual is that there was someone, Mark, who actually had the vision to see an opportunity, and the energy to try to get funding for it. How many opportunities have been lost because the person who sees them just doesn't see the point? They think, and they may be quite right, that there's no point asking because the answer will be no. The next time Mark sees an interesting opportunity, will he be more or less likely to pursue it?

So why did the accounting firm say no to this nice little possibility? Is it because they didn't have time to think about it? Hardly. They are accountants, after all. Once Mark has presented the proposition, it takes about one second to see that it's a good one. It's more likely that this is an example of the rule of thumb which takes on a life of its own.

Here is a more likely explanation of what happened. The original rule was something like: 'It really helps us to know a year in advance what the firm's profit will be, because that profit is our personal income, and we have commitments in our private lives. We therefore have a budget and should not spend in excess of it.' This seems logical and responsible, but a step in the logic has been suppressed. Why does not spending over budget help guarantee us the income we expect? There is an unstated middle step in the argument which must be something like: 'Extra expenditure depresses profit, because it doesn't raise revenues.' Add this in the middle and you now have a logically watertight argument. The only problem is that it is a perfect argument based on false premises. 'Always stay within budget' is a good rule if it's true that 'Extra costs never generate extra revenue.'

This assumption clearly doesn't hold water here – spending £1,000 would pretty quickly generate several times that in revenue. What we have here is a knee-jerk reaction: extra costs = lower profits = bad. It's both untrue in fact and faulty in logic, but that doesn't make any difference. The partners making the decision couldn't question their logic because they weren't conscious of going through a logical process. As they made this stupid decision, saying goodbye to several thousand pounds of effortless quick profit, they probably had a pleasant feeling of acting prudently and responsibly.

So it comes down to logic. I don't expect to be hailed as a great philosopher for this brief analysis – I think the ancient Greeks had the area pretty well covered. The real question is this: the tools you need to avoid this sort of error have been in existence for more than 2,000 years, but what do you need to do to make sure you use them when they are needed?

There is a particular technique for taking more intelligent budget decisions, the ROI rule, which I will deal with in a moment. But there is an even simpler, more powerful technique which will deal with this and many, many other errors. Just ask why.

See what happens in this case:

'We cannot spend outside the budget.'
    'Why not?'
    'Because we need the greatest possible certainty of meeting our budgeted profit figure.'
    'Why does saying no to this proposal reduce our chances of meeting the budgeted profit figure, when it seems almost certain to generate revenues several times the cost?'
    'Errmm . . .'

Again, none of this is going to go down in the annals of philosophy. Why is it so hard to ask why? I can think of a couple of reasons. Neither of them is valid, but they are powerful.

The first reason people find it difficult to ask why is because by the time most people reach positions of authority in organisations, they have also become parents. This means that for years their children have been driving them mad asking, 'Why, why, why?' about everything. Sometimes it's because they genuinely want to know, in which case the poor parent needs a thorough grounding in physics, chemistry, biology, sociology, psychology, history, philosophy, theology and a dozen other disciplines not yet recognised by academia. Sometimes it's just a means of resistance: 'Why can't I have another cake? Why not?' Either way, asking why acquires some rather unfortunate associations.

The second reason people don't ask why as often as they usefully could is that they substitute group consensus for individual thought, as we saw in Chapter 1 with the experiment with the three lines, or the example of the fall of communism: 'x million people can't be wrong.'

In the area of budgets, as in so many areas, taking the

time to ask why gives you power. You can use that power in three ways:

- ◐ Obnoxiously asking why on every occasion, annoying and embarrassing your superiors, reminding them of their five-year-old children in one of their more difficult moods and generally achieving no good for yourself or anyone else.
- ◐ Subtly and with discretion, applying your newfound power to identify missed opportunities and hidden traps, developing powers of persuasion to bring people along with you on better courses of action.
- ◐ Completely privately, using the power of why and superior logic to boost your personal effectiveness in ways that you decline to share with anyone except maybe a chosen few.

HOW FOCUS ON PERFORMANCE DESTROYS PERFORMANCE

I once worked with a software company. At budget time I asked the UK Country Manager what the sales forecast for the next year was. '£2.3m,' he replied, 'but we're working on getting it down to £2.1m.' Down? Wouldn't you want to work on getting it up?

At the same time, the company could see that it was going to meet its annual budget with the deals it had already signed up. The Chief Executive started taking active steps to delay any further sales until the next accounting year. Why would you not sign up a deal as soon as you can, and avoid the risk of losing it? And why, when cashflow was as tight as it was, would you want to delay receiving large sums?

The place was a madhouse. But, as in so many cases, the road to madness was a path of perfect logic, starting from some apparently reasonable premises.

In fact, the two basic premises for the software company were these:

- ❍ We expect a very high level of certainty that we will meet the budget.
- ❍ We take a very firm line with people or units who underperform.

On the face of it there is nothing perverse about either of these, but it is not hard to see how they lead to the madhouse.

The fact is, *certainty comes at the expense of performance*. Put another way, the more you hold me to my guarantee of what I will produce, the less I will offer you. And, perhaps even worse, the less candid I will be about what I could offer you. I may see some fabulous opportunities out there, but if I fear that you will hold me to achieving them on pain of death, I will do my best to make sure that you never get to hear of them. This is the logic of the crazy person at the start of the chapter – 'I won't apply for the really good school, in case I don't get in.'

That was what was going on in this company, and it is very typical. There was a very strong expectation that budgets would be met, and that people would be held to account if they fell short. Reasonably enough, then, people wanted to set their budgets as low as possible. For example, the sales forecast was divided into two parts, 'forecast' and 'pipeline'. The idea was that 'forecast' represented the deals that were reasonably concrete and likely to happen, while 'pipeline' was opportunities at an earlier stage which might or might not come to fruition. A colleague of mine asked one of the salesmen about the criteria for moving a deal from pipeline to forecast. 'They are really the same thing,' he was told. 'It's just that if a deal is in forecast and it dies, you get whacked, so we try to avoid moving deals there until we absolutely have to.'

You could argue that this was a relatively harmless

piece of game-playing, but it has some deadly serious consequences.

The first consequence is that it kills any chance of a candid, useful discussion about the potential of any part of the business. Let's discuss what we could really do with the UK business. How could we sell more to our existing customers? Who isn't buying from us who might, and how do we convince them? Could we expand our market from just banks at present to insurance companies, or fund managers, or hedge funds? This is exactly the sort of discussion you should be having, but can't. Every time I, as UK Country Manager, come up with a good idea for growing sales, my thought is not 'excellent' but 'what happens if this becomes one of my objectives and I fall short?' It's a one-way bet; heads I lose, tails I don't win.

The second consequence is that it positively incentivises people to spend mental energy constructing arguments for their part of the business having less potential than it actually does. This is a criminal waste of energy. This sort of thinking is hard, and you should focus it on finding ways of improving, not diminishing, your business.

The third consequence is that it sets up an opposition between management and those managed. Now, there is always going to be some tension between the people who produce the results and the people who manage them, set their targets and evaluate and reward them, but it makes sense to avoid aggravating those tensions when you can.

This focus on performance also explained why the Chief Executive was trying to suppress sales at the end of the year. Once he had met budget, he was safe. Additional revenue was better off in the next year, where it gave him a head start on next year's budget, than added to the current year. There was a complete divergence between his interests as an individual and the interests of the company. For the company, suppressing sales was stupid and risky. There was a risk that they would be lost altogether. Maybe the customers' budgets would be cut, or there would be a change of top management who didn't see that system as a priority, or the board would decree a company-wide spending freeze – anyone who knows anything about sales knows how many things can derail sales before they are signed. Even if nothing like this happened, the customers could understandably become frustrated with a company which had spent months, if not years, selling to them, only to slow down inexplicably as they approached the critical point.

HOW BUDGETS ENCOURAGE OVERSPENDING

When I was Commercial Director of a marketing consultancy, we used to do very well out of advance payments. At one point we had the equivalent of one third of a year's turnover in the bank for work we hadn't yet done. When it came to funding our growth, we received much more help from our clients than we did from our bank. This was great for us, but maybe less so for our clients. We did particularly well towards the end of the year. Every October I would ask the account managers to contact all their clients and ask them if they had any money they wanted to spend before the end of the year. This generally produced a good response, the best ever being this: 'Please send us an invoice for £200,000, with some vague description of work. It *must* be with us before the end of December, otherwise we lose the budget. We can talk in the new year about what you do for it.'

Just as a budget will prevent you from seizing unexpected opportunities, it will encourage you to spend money to little purpose, simply because it is expected. If budgeted money isn't spent by the end of the year, it's generally lost. Even worse, since so many budgets are based on last year's spending, not spending an amount one year can make it harder to get budget in the subsequent year.

HOW BUDGETS STOP YOU THINKING ABOUT THE FUTURE

This seems strange. Isn't the whole point of budgeting to look to the future? Well no, unless by 'the future' you mean 'the immediate future, that is, the future in which we sort of assume nothing much is going to change'.

The thing about constructing the future is:

1 It involves spending money over more than one year, and almost always spending more in year one than you receive.

2 It works to its own timescale, not the arbitrary duration of an accounting year.

3 It is inherently uncertain, with a level of uncertainty which is not acceptable in a budgeting process.

To illustrate conflict between budgeting and building the future, take an example from my past life, in a large media group. The group at the time was not noted for its strategic dynamism, and decided that it wanted to do better. It therefore launched a new process – the operating plan. The idea was this: 'Show us, first, what you would expect, over the next three years, in your business if you just continue doing what you are doing. Then give us some ideas for new developments. For each of these, show us the costs and revenues involved, again over three years. Then we as a group can see all the different investment opportunities open to us, and choose between them. If we choose one of yours, then we will let you do it.'

It was a very sensible process, but it was totally overwhelmed by the budgeting process. The operating plan was supposed to be submitted a month before the normal budget. This raised the obvious problem – what happens if the first year of the operating plan looks different from the budget, which covers the same period? Clearly this wasn't acceptable, so the first year of the operating plan had to be done in the same way, to the same level of detail, as the budget.

Most of the attention went on the first year, because it was going to turn into a budget commitment. Because everyone was in a 'budgeting' frame of mind – detailed, cautious, and very much grounded in current reality – the more speculative ideas for the later years never really stood a chance. We ended up doing the budget a month earlier and hardly paying any attention to the future of the business. It should have been completely the other way round: look at the investment possibilities for the next three years, decide which you want to do, then make sure that the next year's budget has a proper allowance for the investment you have decided to make. How long does it take to review a whole range of exciting new opportunities, pick out the best, and plan them to a sufficient level of detail that you can budget their first year? Certainly more than the month that this process allowed. The budget won, the future was lost.

HOW BUDGETS INSPIRE 'RECKLESS CAUTION'

How can caution be reckless? When you are suffering from tunnel vision, or a severely limited time horizon. The problem arises when you allow your thinking to be dominated by the next year. You can always improve results and reduce risk there by holding back on investment. In the short term, this works fine. In the long term, it's fatal. Chapter 3 on cost cutting tells the story of the battery company Berec who boosted results in the short term by cutting back on product development.

The first thing you need is a change of perception. In

this case, you don't need mind-altering drugs. A simple picture will do it:

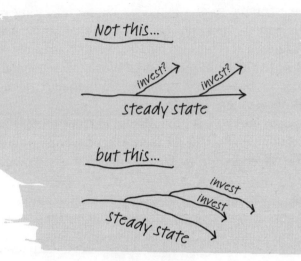

The basic false assumption that makes reckless caution appear attractive is that there is a steady state for the business. While we have options to invest, we assume, tacitly, that if we don't do anything particularly novel then things will continue much as they are. Be clear, though, that if you don't do anything in particular, things still change. And they change for the worse. Ask yourself: what forces are at work to undermine my steady state? And what are at work to support it? Consider technological change, actions of existing competitors, emergence of new competitors, economic changes, demographic changes, etc. I suspect that the first list will be much longer than the second.

If you need to reinforce the message, do this. Think back five years. Which were your top products, favourite customers? Where are they now? Probably much reduced.

Project forwards, using the same rate of decay. There may be an argument for assuming a faster rate of decay. I would be surprised if there is an argument for using a slower one. (If you can't remember the top customers or products from five years ago, your point is proven.)

There is a horrible psychological paradox at work here. In times of rapid and confusing change, or times of economic stress, the familiar is more than ever under threat. And yet it is exactly in those times that, instinctively, the status quo feels more and more attractive, and change (self-initiated change, that is, not reaction to events) more and more threatening.

You could look at it as an exercise in creative paranoia. And, as Andy Grove of Intel famously observed, only the paranoid survive.

SEPARATE BUDGETING AND PLANNING

Lots of organisations like to group budgeting and planning together, but that is part of the problem. Budgeting is very detail-oriented, while thinking about the future is much more broad-brush. When you are budgeting, you worry about whether you have the new sales manager starting in the right month. In thinking about the future, you worry about whether a particular market exists or not. These are two completely different frames of minds. If you wanted to be extreme, you might say that different people ought to be doing them. In practice, this will almost always be unrealistic. Try as far as possible to put together a team of detail people and broad-brush people, and closely monitor the balance between them. In budgeting, the detail people should be leading. In thinking about the future, they should be following.

PUT BUDGETING AT THE SERVICE OF THE LONG TERM

There is an inevitable, necessary tension between the short term, where the budget belongs, and the long term.

However much we might want to believe the contrary, improving, or even preserving, the business in the future means some sacrifice of short-term profit. In this struggle between long term and short term, the budget has advantages. It is more detailed, and hence more credible. Long-term plans are hedged about with worrying uncertainty, while the budget is rooted in today. It inspires more confidence.

You can spend forever tweaking a budget, fussing over every last detail, while the longer-term future is less clear. Budgets are easier to relate to today's actions.

If you are going to make sure that you won't sacrifice the long to the short term, you need to give serious thought to the way you handle the two.

Do the long-term plan first. If you deal with budgets in September or October, try to have longer-term plans settled well before you start. This probably means working on them in the spring. Whatever you do, don't try to do them together.

Separate out current expenditure and longer-term investment. That is, put them on different sheets, or in different lines of budget. If you have one line for, say, marketing, and it includes both the marketing which supports the existing business and that which develops a new market, then your fledgling market doesn't stand a chance. At the first little bit of pressure, out comes the development money. Current revenues aren't affected, and everyone is happy.

USE THE RETURN ON INVESTMENT RULE

I owe this rule to Mike, a venture capitalist who sat on the board of a company where I was Finance Director. He spent most of the board meetings listening hard, only speaking up when someone said we needed to spend some money. Then he reminded us of the Return on Investment Rule:

'Any money you spend is an investment. You don't spend money because it is in the budget. You don't spend it because you spent the same amount last year. You don't spend it because Fred has resigned and you need to replace him with someone on a similar salary. You spend money because it produces a return.'

This rule is quite profound in its simplicity, and can be applied in many different circumstances. Going back to our earlier case study, it would have dealt very rapidly with the decision about whether Mark should spend some more money on advertising his tax planning software. It will also help you reduce costs much more intelligently, if that is what you need to do. Sometimes it will tell you to spend less money, but other times it will tell you that you should be spending *more*.

Try this unusual exercise – go through every line of your budget and ask: 'What would this area have to do for me to make me want to spend *more* here, not less?'

The rule suggests that you shouldn't have a marketing budget at all. You should have a marketing investment assessment process. Look for as many opportunities as you can to spend marketing money in ways that produce a positive return, and do them all. Amazon used to do this. They knew it made sense for them to pay up to $33 to acquire a new customer. If anyone could offer them a source of new customers which delivered for $33 or less, they had a deal. Amazon would buy all the customers they were offered. Was Amazon inside or outside of its marketing budget, if it even had one?

The question is irrelevant, because it knew that any money it spent was well spent. I had a similar discussion with a medical equipment firm. They had had good results at a trade show the previous year by not just waiting on their stand, but sending two people through the halls to accost likely looking prospects. On the basis of this, they were thinking of sending three people the next year. I asked how many prospects were likely to be at the show, and we realised that even three people would be barely scratching the surface. It would have made sense to send ten.

To use the ROI rule, you will need to change the role of your finance department. Instead of being the budget police, they need to become small-scale in-house venture capitalists. They evaluate proposals for investment and, for the ones that pass the test, are responsible for finding the money.

SEPARATE EXPECTATIONS, NEEDS AND POSSIBILITIES

These are separate things:

- An expectation is what I think will happen.
- A possibility is what could happen, or what I really want to happen.
- A need is what must happen.

In the context of a budget, we might say:

- We have to make at least £1m this year otherwise we are in trouble (need).
- I think we could realistically make £1.2m (expectation).
- We might have a chance of doing £1.4m (possibility).

Put like this, it seems simple, almost embarrassingly so. And yet, how many budgets actually recognise the three different numbers? The same budgets try to make one number serve all three purposes, with predictably depressing results. The people who will be held to the budget put their efforts into lowering expectations as close as possible to the minimum needed, and nobody even thinks about possibilities.

Recognise uncertainty, to the point of looking at needs, expectations and possibilities, and the budgeting process could start to do you some good.

CHAPTER 6

HELPFUL MAXIMS

HOW DO YOU CHOOSE A RULE OF THUMB?

We need rules of thumb, because we don't have time to work everything out from scratch. In the film *Up In the Air*, the character played by George Clooney is at the airport, looking for the fastest check-in line. He joins the line behind a group of Chinese people. He explains to his companion why he chose that line: 'Asians travel efficiently.' She reproaches him for racial prejudice. 'I'm like my mother,' he replies. 'I stereotype. It saves time.' In this case he is being sensible, as the whole point of this character is that he spends his entire life on the road, in and out of airports, and so has had the chance to observe what happens.

I have my own rules of thumb, similarly derived from experience. I know that the total cost of a restaurant meal is very consistently 2.5 to 3 times the cost of the main course. When travelling in India, where bus timetables didn't seem to exist, I worked out that, over flat roads, buses did a very consistent 40 kilometres per hour and journey times were in fact very predictable.

All these are rules of thumb derived from personal experience and observation, and they are helpful. The danger arises when we adopt other people's rules. These may be left over from a older epoch, or developed in very different circumstances, or even worse, they might appeal more because they sound good than because they actually work. There is in fact a large body of what you could almost call the folk wisdom of business, which appeals for reasons which have nothing to do with efficacy. These are the maxims and rules of thumb that we need to beware of, and there is no shortage of them. I am going to run through a long list of them, but I can't hope to be comprehensive. That's why I will also cover the Six Pillars of Really Bad Ideas, that is, the six most frequent ways in which bad ideas can appeal. Remember these, and you can begin to spot when a neat aphorism is leading you astray.

If It Ain't Broke, Don't Fix It

This is usually a bad idea, if applied to anything important. Even if it ain't broke, someone somewhere is working to break it. Successful companies make sure that they never forget this. Look at the two companies who have made the most money, for the longest time, in the computer business: Intel and Microsoft. As I've mentioned previously, it was Andy Grove, when head of Intel, who observed that 'only the paranoid survive'. Kevin Turner, Chief Operating Officer of Microsoft, recently described the 'healthy level of insecurity' which drives Microsoft's constant innovation. Microsoft's PC operating system business isn't broken – at the time of writing they're shipping vast quantities of Windows 7 – but Microsoft is working very hard on developing its presence in cloud computing, which could eventually wipe out the conventional Windows system.

Even if nobody is actively working to break your product or service, everything has a natural life. It follows an S-curve:

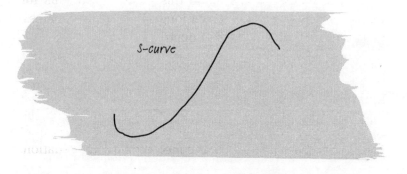

S-curve

Any product, job or company starts small, then grows to maturity, then begins to decline. In some industries this is very obvious. At Intel, for instance, 90% of December revenue comes from products that were not shipping in January. The corollary of that is that 90% of their revenue in January comes from products that will be dead by the end of the year. At Intel they have no illusions on this front – the existing business needs to be recreated every year.

The danger comes when the evolution of the business is slower. That is when the risk arises. Two years is a long time in business, and five years is an eternity. If the pace of change is such that significant change is only visible over two or more years, you will need to make a conscious effort to expand your perspective.

Look back far enough, and you'll see that everything you or your predecessors were doing is now dead. Then look forward – everything you are doing now will also die. The question is, do you wait until it starts to die, or work on the next thing while your current business is still going strong? Myself, if I have to build a new business, I'd rather do it while my current business is going well, money is plentiful and confidence high.

The 'If it ain't broke' principle is fundamentally a recipe for complacency, for settling for good enough, not as good as possible. We've been very forcibly reminded recently that times can change, and good enough can pretty quickly become no good at all. Up until 2008 we had a long period of economic growth, and growth can hide a lot of mediocrity. The recession has made this painfully obvious for many people. If you care about longevity in your business, good enough just isn't good enough.

What's the antidote? You may well hear yourself, or someone else, actually saying the 'It ain't broke, don't fix it' maxim, in which case you know you need to pause for a moment and make sure it still makes sense. Much of the time, though, you don't hear yourself thinking, 'It ain't broke, I won't fix it.' This is the more dangerous situation.

Here are two techniques for working out when something is about to break, and whether you need to do anything about it.

The first uses the invaluable S-curve already mentioned. Take all your activities, or all your products, or all your customers, and locate them on the curve. A good distribution looks something like this:

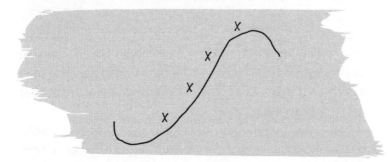

There are some new products coming up, securing the future. There are some products in the middle of their lives, which are generating nice profits. Then there are some products coming to the end of their lives. They are probably declining in volume, which gives you the opportunity to make them seriously profitable for a little while, in effect by 'breaking' them. They will be finished soon, so you can take some decisive action in the knowledge that the worst it will do is accelerate the process. You can afford to take a very hard line on pricing; any customers still using these almost-obsolete products are probably very attached to them, and many of your competitors have stopped making them. Alternatively, you could cut back on marketing support for these end-of-life products. It saves money, and these products aren't gaining new customers anyway. They are almost broken.

On the other hand, if the picture looks like this, you have more of a problem.

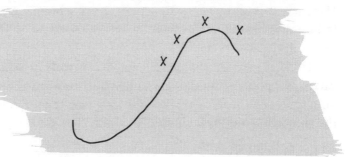

Everything is at the end of its life. There are no new products coming up, and no reliable earners to see you through the next few years. This is an emergency which doesn't feel like an emergency. Nothing is broken yet, but everything is about to break.

I hope that, when you draw the the S-curve of your business, it doesn't look anything like the second one. To be sure that you never end up in that position, draw the picture as is, and then project forward a few years. Simply move everything a few years to the right and then what does it look like? Now you know what you need to be doing, now, to secure the future with new products or new customers.

If It Is Broke, Don't Fix It

There are lots of reasons why trying to fix something that's 'broke' could be a bad idea (there are some good reasons why it could be a good thing though, so be careful).

There is a very important question to ask before you decide to fix anything. *What would I be doing if I weren't spending time trying to fix this situation?*

You could be:

● Building something new.
● Reinforcing something that already works.
● Taking preventive action to fix something that is about to break. (Maybe in the time it takes you fix one thing you could prevent three things from breaking.)

You would need to know that the thing is actually fixable. Sometimes this is a problem with new products which aren't doing well. They are not working, but did they ever work? Do they have any chance of ever working? If a project or product is dear to our hearts, it is easy to obsess about trying to get it to work, even long past the point when an objective observer would conclude that there was no point, or no chance of it ever working as it should.

One common error is trying to fix things that used to work, but no longer do so. Trying harder somehow seems an easier option than thinking harder. Thinking harder might reveal evidence that the world had changed, that the approach needed to change, or that a completely new approach was needed. Sometimes the pain involved is psychological. If we built the current business, it may feel more like 'killing our own children' than 'reinventing ourselves'.

I encountered one of these situations while director of a marketing consultancy. As I have mentioned previously, our speciality was helping pharmaceutical companies develop marketing messages for new products using their clinical data. In the early 1980s this was a radical idea, almost black magic. Nobody knew quite how it worked, but everybody wanted it. By the late 1980s the mystery had gone, but it was still a high-level service that commanded a good fee. By the mid-1990s the mystique had evaporated. The service was seen as a commodity, and the companies that provided it found themselves selling not to marketing managers who were interested in value, but to professional purchasing agents who just wanted the lowest price. At the same time, there were fewer new projects (the pharmaceutical companies couldn't come up with new products) and the emphasis was moving from clinical communication (promoting to doctors who neither knew nor cared what the drugs cost) to pharmacoeconomics (convincing economists and accountants who now controlled prescribing decisions that your drug offered the best return on investment).

With the benefit of hindsight, the conclusion was clear. The party was over. We had to reinvent ourselves as pharmacoeconomics communications consultants, or shut up shop.

That's not what we did, of course. We redoubled our efforts at what had made us successful in the past. We worked harder. We worked longer. We recruited more sales people. By that I mean we recruited more expensive sales people (and, wow, they were getting more expensive, as every firm in the industry was trying to grow its sales force). We made more calls. We got on more planes. We invested more in pitches – but to no avail . . .

It's not just companies that make this mistake. Whole countries can do the same. Think of the UK in the 1960s and 70s. It was enjoying a flood of cash from its oil reserves in the North Sea, but what was it doing with the money? Trying desperately to prop up dying industries which had had their day: coal, shipbuilding, cars, bulk steel – industries which had made the country great, but which others could now do better or cheaper. It didn't work, of course. No amount of government money could resist the economic forces at work. It could only delay the inevitable, and make the industrial carnage of the early 1980s all the worse. What would the UK be now if it had invested all that subsidy in industries of the future?

So, how do you tell when it's time to cut your losses and shift your efforts elsewhere?

Here are some ways to avoid becoming fixated on failures:

- ▶ *Adopt a rule of 'only fix it once'.* If something isn't working, you are allowed to try to fix it. If it still doesn't work, abandon it and move on.
- ▶ *Think about opportunity cost.* Quantify it. If you are struggling to fix something, look at the time and money you are spending on it and write down the best

alternative use for it. Does that look more attractive? If it does, then do that instead.

❍ *Look out for the point of diminishing returns.* This can be a very good clue that something is broken beyond the point that it can be economically fixed. In the marketing consultancy, for example, the real clue was that our sales efforts were running into diminishing returns. It needed more and more sales people making more and more calls to generate the same number of opportunities to propose, and more and more investment in pitches even to be credible, never mind win the business.

❍ *Set clear milestones for success.* When you start a new project, be clear not just what success looks like, but what the first indications of success are. Let's say that success is 'selling 10,000 units per month after three years'. Three years is a long time to wait. Is there some earlier milestone you should set? Maybe your target should be 'selling 1,000 units per month after nine months' or 'being adopted by five existing customers within one year'. It can be hard enough to abort a project that is clearly failing, but much harder to kill something that is clearly heading for failure. Having clearly predetermined milestones makes it easier.

❍ *Try to minimise emotional investment.* Peter Drucker put his finger on it when he invented a classification of products including the category of 'investments in managerial ego'. The last thing you want to do is end up with your ego, or your prestige or reputation, attached to a failing project. There is a tricky balance here – you and others need to make some emotional investment in a project or else it will never move, but too much and you could become blinded to the reality.

Constantly remind yourself – ignore sunk costs:

- Project A requires an investment of £1m in the next year and will produce a return of £1.2m.
- Project B requires an investment of £1m in the next year and will produce a return of £2m.

Should it matter that Project A has already had £5m spent on it (prior to it producing any return) while Project B has had nothing spent on it so far? It shouldn't, but often it does. The logic is inescapable, but the psychology is trickier. Behavioural economists know that the value we attach to something depends a lot on what we had to pay to acquire it, regardless of its value in the future.

Take Massive Action Now

This is superficially appealing, but its appeal is based on two common pillars of Bad Ideas:

1. Magical Thinking
2. The Feelgood Factor

There's an appealing magical quality to the idea that if we want to solve a problem we can just apply massive action. Thought, planning, the choice of appropriate means, the analysis of possibilities and risk, the analysis of whether the result is worth the effort? No need.

It also makes us feel good. Action, particularly if dramatic and painful, is good.

The only problem is, this is the logic of the First World War. Not winning the war? Throw more men into the slaughter. Strategy now working? No, so do yet more of the same.

The answer is really very simple. Make sure you have a plan. As you start to act, pause occasionally to check that the results are arising as you thought they would. If not, stop or redirect your action.

Failure is Not an Option

What does it mean when someone says this? If it is just 'failure would be a really, really bad thing here,' then it's just a truism, but mostly when you hear this there's something else. There's an element of magical thinking, an idea that we can select a small number of projects and choose that they absolutely, positively will not fail. It harks back to fairy stories and legends where you had a magic flag which you waved, or a magic horn that you blew to receive strange help. The catch was that you could only use it once, or maybe three times.

Magical thinking is a wonderful thing for fairy tales, but its track record in the real world is not encouraging. Refusing to countenance the possibility of failure can actually make failure more likely, in a number of ways.

- ◗ *It creates rigidity.* We have to stick to the plan, because to modify it would be 'failure', which is not an option in this case. Ultimately we fail in front of the possibility of success, because success doesn't look the way it should.
- ◗ *It creates blindness.* There are forces at work which we cannot control – competitors, changes in technology, or changes in the needs of our customers. Some of these may cause us to 'fail'. If we cannot recognise the possibility of failure, then we cannot look clearly at what is going on in these areas. We ignore reality until it really bites us.
- ◗ *It creates concealment and dishonesty.* Many times clients have asked me to rescue projects which are failing, or have failed. Almost invariably, these projects had been failing for some time before senior management became aware that anything was wrong. Those managing the project knew that they were in trouble, but spent months trying to cover up.

It may seem paradoxical, but the best way to ensure against failure is to accept that it's a possibility. Avoid the magical thinking, and engage with reality. Then you can do some sensible things:

- Be sensitive to the early warning signs.
- Communicate candidly about risks.
- Plan alternatives.
- Cut your losses earlier if things go bad.
- Recognise alternative forms of success.

Just Do It

It's a brilliant slogan. It has sold countless billions of pounds' worth of sports kit for Nike. It's also popular in the organisational world, where it exemplifies the belief that with sufficient will, courage and determination, anything is possible. Heady stuff. Just one problem, though. It doesn't work.

The funny thing is that the slogan is associated with elite athletes, but when you look at what those athletes actually do, it's the very opposite of 'just do it'. Nobody gets up in the morning, girds their loins, 'just goes' to the Olympics and 'just runs' a marathon.

They have detailed training plans, setting out exactly what they need to do each day in the months or years leading up to the event.

They have a whole supporting cast of trainers, coaches, physiotherapists, nutritionists and psychologists who help them to prepare.

They focus. If you plan to run the marathon at the next Olympics, you concentrate on that. You don't try to learn the piano and start a business at the same time.

So here are some questions for anyone who feels tempted to apply 'just do it' in their organisation.

Do you have a plan? Do you actually know the steps you need to go through to get to the desired result? Are you being realistic about the amount of time you need to build the capabilities you need?

Are you providing people with the support they need to succeed? If elite athletes need a large supporting cast to perform at their best then so too does your, probably more ordinary, team.

Are you sufficiently focused? It's tempting to launch a 'just do it' initiative this week, then another one next week, then another one the month after that. You need to be realistic about how much time people have, and how many different objectives they can handle at the same time. Be honest with yourself and admit that it's less than you would ideally like.

'Just do it' is tempting. It's inspiring, but in the end it's a form of magical thinking.

What's the alternative? Any time you find yourself saying 'just do it' to yourself, just ask yourself the following three questions:

○ Do I have a plan, and do I have grounds for believing that my plan might work?
○ Do I have the necessary skills and knowledge?
○ Do I have access to the necessary support?

If you are saying 'just do it' to someone else, then you absolutely must explore these questions with them.

Time Management

Time management is a huge industry – books, seminars, software products and any number of clever diaries and organisers. The industry has something in common with the weight-loss business and much of the self-help and self-improvement business. It's sustained by a dirty little secret which, once you take a moment to look at, isn't a secret: *time management is a huge industry because it doesn't work*. Contrast it with a much smaller industry which does work – cycle training. Most people learn to ride a bike themselves, or from friends or parents or older siblings. They might have a few lessons, probably more about safety than actually riding, but it's no big deal. Anybody who wants to ride a bike manages to learn pretty easily. That's the paradox; time management is a much bigger industry than cycle training because cycle training satisfies its customers and time management does not.

I've been on a time-management course. You've been on a time-management course. I'd guess that just about everybody reading this book has been on a time-management course (the publisher has limited distribution in the further reaches of the Amazon rainforest, which is about the only place one can still find a few primitive tribes who have not been on time-management courses or owned a personal organiser). And yet, how much good did it do?

My experience of a time-management seminar was surreal. Our Managing Director had taken the whole company to a central London hotel for a full day of very slick, very nicely packaged, very expensive time-management training. After every break, the whole group was late starting while she finished off the phone calls she was making. Guess how much we improved as a company as a result of our day out?

And yet, time management remains a major issue. Several times in my troubleshooting days I was brought in to take over from a finance director who had failed, and been fired. Time management, I found, was always a large part of the problem. I remember one session during the handover process when I spent hours with the outgoing FD and the financial accountant going through the statutory accounts in minute detail. It seemed to me that the financial accountant was the only one who knew what it was all about, and that he was perfectly capable of dealing with things on his own. It was a painful session for me, partly because it was so boring, but more because there was a voice at the back of my head saying something like, 'We have a real problem collecting cash from customers. The system is broken and if we don't fix it then, under the new banking agreements, the investors need to put their hands in their pockets to the tune of many millions of pounds. Shouldn't we be spending time on that?'

Turnaround professionals, whose basic selling point is that they are successful where other people have failed, operate on the principle that you must never have more than three priorities. The principle has certainly worked for me; usually one of the first things I did on turnaround assignments was to go through my predecessor's diary and cancel meetings, decline to attend other meetings, cancel non-essential projects and withdraw from participation in other projects. Then I could start to do something useful. Why does it need a crisis?

Nancy Reagan's Solution to the Time-management Problem

Forget priority A/B/C, forget urgent vs important, throw away your organiser and uninstall your software. The wife of former president Ronald Reagan has the answer to all time-management woes, and it's brilliantly simple:

'Just Say No'

Nancy was actually thinking about drug abuse when she launched this brilliant maxim, but it applies just as well to time abuse.

❶ Just say no to low-value activities.
❷ Just say no to things that other people can do better.
❸ Just say no to complicated solutions.

Nancy's method has support from other gurus with stronger credentials in the management world, too.

Peter Drucker even invented a special (rather ugly) word for it. He wrote that just as you as your prioritise some tasks, you should 'posteriorise' others. This is a euphemism for 'don't do them'. It's interesting to speculate why Drucker, who usually wrote so clearly and so directly, needed to invent an ugly euphemism in this case. We will come back to this point later.

Fellow management expert Tom Peters urges you to create a 'to-do' list and a 'to-don't' list. It's the same idea.

The point they are both making is this. If your list of things to do is too long to do them all effectively, then simply reorganising or reclassifying the list isn't going to help. You will need to drop things off the list.

The solution is clear. But it hasn't solved your problem yet, has it?

Why Nancy's Brilliant Solution Doesn't Work

The thing about the 'just say no' solution as applied to avoiding drug abuse was that it was clear, commonsensical and completely compelling *to the sort of person who was at no risk of getting into drug abuse anyway*. If you were at risk for sociological or psychological reasons, or already addicted, then it was no help at all.

The same is true when it comes to applying the solution to the problem of time abuse. Rationally it's dead easy, but if we want to find a way of applying it we need to delve into the politics, the sociology and the psychology of you and your organisation.

The Real Reason for Time Abuse

Why is it so difficult to say no? Is it because, as many people would plead, their bosses just won't allow it? I don't believe this. Anyone who has worked in an organisation knows that everyone has a whole repertoire of techniques for not doing what they don't want to do, even if the boss wants it done. Passive resistance, delay, confusion, distraction and misdirection abound. Anyone who has ever managed anyone else knows that people are endlessly skilled in doing what they want to do, not what you want them to.

The question is more why they choose to do things that don't make them effective, that leave them stressed and overworked, and that in some cases lead to them failing and getting fired. Think, for instance, of the finance director I mentioned earlier, picking over the technicalities of the annual accounts instead of dealing with a serious operational issue. He couldn't claim boss pressure as a reason for this; the chief executive had no interest whatsoever in annual accounts, but was jumping up and down screaming about the problem with collecting cash.

No, sorry, 'they won't let me do it differently' won't wash. For every time abuser who is running into trouble by being too eager to please, there are ten who are stubbornly ploughing their own furrow, regardless of what it does for their boss, their colleagues, their careers or their sanity.

Why is this? Why so much irrational behaviour? Once again, to answer the question requires us to abandon ordinary logic in favour of psychological logic. Here I apply my mathematical training. If a problem is too hard, it's probably because you have it framed incorrectly. Often, reframing it makes the problem simple. In this case, the right-hand diagram makes the solution obvious.

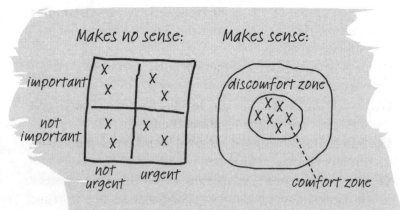

Time-management gurus advise us to classify our tasks into urgent or not urgent and important or not important. Then we are supposed to concentrate our efforts on the important, giving particular attention to the important but not urgent. Sound advice, but when you plot most people's activities on the matrix, as in the diagram on the left, they are all over the place.

If, however, we adopt a different framework the picture makes complete sense. Forget the rational, results-oriented way of classifying tasks, and instead look at the emotional dimension. Now all is clear. The real time-management principle is revealed as: *spend as much time as possible within my comfort zone.*

Comfort zone activities include such things as:

- Things I am really good at (even if they are irrelevant).
- Things I did in the past that made me successful (even if they won't make me successful in my new job, now).
- Things that have no emotional content (technical accounting matters, reorganising the filing system).
- Things that don't really matter (because nobody will care, or even notice, if I don't do them well).
- Anything that distracts me from tasks in the 'discomfort zone.

Discomfort zone activities include such things as:

- Things subject to high levels of uncertainty and ambiguity (like thinking about the future).
- Things involving interpersonal conflict (dealing with underperforming members of the team).
- New challenges, i.e., things I haven't done before (because I might not be very good at them the first time I try, and as an experienced manager I am very heavily invested in being good at everything I do).
- Things that could have very bad consequences if they

go wrong (which is, when you think of it, almost the definition of an important decision or project).

So, fundamentally, time abuse is a way of managing anxiety. We concentrate our time on activities which don't cause us anxiety. We may even use comfortable activities as ways of distracting ourselves from the less comfortable ones.

The Real Key to Time Management

- ▶ It has nothing to do with technology, although the personal organisers and software will help once you have dealt with the big issue.
- ▶ It has nothing to do with technique. It's not exactly difficult to distinguish between the urgent and the important or to make lists of what you need to do, but the challenge is to act on that knowledge.
- ▶ It's not about being clear about priorities. If we dared to look, we would very easily see what those were.

No, the real key to time management is to manage your anxiety so that you can see what you are trying to ignore and do what you know you should be doing.

So how do you manage anxiety? The first step is to understand it better; in fact, to make friends with it. We tend to treat anxiety as a bad thing, something to be avoided. In excess, it is a bad thing, and can even need professional help to resolve. Properly managed and channelled, however, anxiety can be one of our most important faculties.

As human beings, we experience anxiety for a purpose. Think about the caveman again, making his way home through a dark forest. He is anxious, and for good reason. There are scary things in the forest. He needs to be anxious to help him stay alive. Anxiety does this in two ways. First, it makes him vigilant. His senses are more acute, and his attention is more focused on what is moving around him in the dark. He doesn't have an iPod, but if he did he would have taken the earphones out and switched it off. Second, the caveman's anxiety makes him respond faster if something dangerous does appear. His muscles are tense, and ready for action.

The world has changed now, but we still have the same responses. We are, after all, descended from the more anxious cavemen and women, the ones whose anxiety gave them a better chance of survival.

There is a form of anticipatory anxiety which can be highly productive. Athletes and performers use it before an important event. It focuses their attention – i.e., please don't talk to me just before I am due to give a speech/ compete in an event.

There is also a 'signal function' of anxiety which is hugely valuable. It doesn't just tell us that something is potentially dangerous, or that something needs our attention. As we move towards the important issues, our anxiety rises. It's a clue that we are heading in the right direction. Try this experiment. Work out what is in your discomfort zone. Make a list of all the things you might do to develop your business, or your career, or your life. Notice which seem comfortable to contemplate, and which are uncomfortable. On the uncomfortable list there will some of the most valuable things you can do.

Now we are making progress, working with anxiety rather than trying to fight it. Don't push things too far, though. Far too often in life we try to push aside the emotional side of life, particularly when we are working in organisations. Don't go charging ahead in the direction of maximum anxiety – you will find yourself falling back. Instead, push gently but steadily in that direction. Remember that it is possible to expand your comfort zone. Pick something a little way outside the current zone and work on it until it becomes comfortable. Then move a little further.

Always Give 110%

If there were one cliché I could nominate for permanent removal from the language, it's this one. I certainly wouldn't recruit anyone using it for a job in finance or anything involving numbers, because it just isn't mathematically possible. The most you can give is 100% – trust me, I have a degree in maths.

Even if you don't take it literally, 'always give 110%' still expresses a confusion which can be highly dangerous. Here's why.

You can't be 'always' at any constant level because, in any job beyond the completely mundane, the level of challenge is always changing. I'm very glad that my local fire brigade don't feel the need to give it even 100% all the time, but in fact spend many hours playing volleyball or drinking tea. I'm reassured that, if I did need to call them, they'd be able to respond immediately with all their energy.

Confusion about arithmetic may promote, or at least help to disguise, real confusion about priorities. I am reminded about the entrepreneur who said she spent '50% of the time looking after customers, 50% looking after staff, and then of course 50% of the time looking after share-holders'. Maybe it's a joke, but it suggests that some difficult choices have not been made.

It confuses input and output. It's not what you're putting in, but what you're achieving. There have been times in my career when, for months on end, I could have, as they say in Hollywood, 'phoned in my performance', but then there have been part-time projects done over a few weeks which have made millions. Obsess on inputs not outputs and you miss this. In fact, the need to be constantly active can create busywork which crowds out the genuinely useful activity.

Want to give it 110%? Please lie down until the urge passes. Then take some time to think, then do something *useful*.

You Can't Get the Staff

'You just can't get the staff,' you hear. Sometimes it's a lament about 'the youth of today', sometimes a complaint about the general bloody-mindedness of the universe. Stop right there. Stop blaming the youth, or the universe. Take a look at yourself and your organisation. That's where the problem is, and that's where you can start to solve it. It could be any of the following:

'*They expect too much.*' Stop blaming 'them'. If people can get a better deal elsewhere, of course they will take it. If you can't match it, that's because your competitors can make more from their employees than you can; maybe they're better organised, or maybe they make better products. Whatever it is, they're doing something that you're not.

You're hunting mythological creatures. It's like the job specification for a finance director that I see regularly, which always makes me laugh: 'strategist . . . command of the big picture . . . absolute mastery of detail'. These things just don't go together – you might as well look for an Olympic weightlifter who could also compete in the gymnastics.

Your non-financial rewards package stinks. Salary may be competitive, but what about the other elements: autonomy, respect, flexibility . . . People aren't stupid, and if your organisation gets a reputation for offering nothing but money, you're going to struggle to attract people.

And finally . . . the really big, scary one. *They just don't want to work with you.* Not your company, you personally. If you're like the MD who got through five procurement managers in two years, you need to take a long, hard look at yourself. What is it about you that makes you impossible to work with?

Often, 'You can't get the staff' sounds a little like, 'I've got this fantastic business plan for turning lead into gold, but I just can't find a philosopher's stone.' There is no philosopher's stone, but the recipe isn't a huge secret:

realism, self-awareness, flexibility and a little humility will get you the people you need.

There is also a very simple, but at the same time very hard, question to answer. To attract the people you need, you need to offer them a better deal – money, excitement, prestige, personal development, whatever – than they can get anywhere else. To be able to do this, and still make a profit, these people need to be more productive in your employ than they are anywhere else. So the question is, how do you ensure that they will be more productive working with you than elsewhere? Investment banks can pay their staff more than anyone else because those staff can generate more money in an investment bank than anywhere else. Google can recruit really top software developers because at Google those developers can produce cooler stuff than they can anywhere else.

Front Office Good, Back Office Bad

This one is a hardy perennial, and is having a great surge of popularity at the time of writing, as the UK government struggles to reduce public spending. Let's take a look at one example of this: the idea that, whether in the public or private sector, we can maintain levels of services or levels of sales while cutting costs if we just protect the 'front line' while cutting the 'back office'.

Why do I hate this idea? Let me count the ways:

Think of how you would apply the logic in a company. The sales function is clearly in the front line, so we protect it while cutting the back office. We can obviously dispense with all those useless paper-pushers and desk jockeys who fritter away their days sending out invoices, getting the invoices paid and making sure that purchasing is scheduled so that we can actually supply what we have sold.

Sometimes the best way to strengthen the front line is to invest in the back office. Think, for instance, of the police, who notoriously used to spend lots of time in the station doing paperwork when they should have been out arresting criminals and reassuring the citizenry. Then there was a move to recruit more civilian staff so that the actual police officers could be seen out and about more. Very sensible, but presumably about to be reversed.

And finally, the ultimate example of how skimping on back office can damage you. It's Barings Bank, broken through the actions of one rogue trader, Nick Leeson, who lost £800m on unauthorised trades. This should never have happened; Leeson should have been stopped almost as soon as he started. The reason he wasn't was that, in contravention of a basic principle which any accountant learns in the first month of their training, Leeson could both trade and account for his trades. This meant he could manipulate the accounts to cover his losses. Why did Barings tolerate this flagrant breach of the basic principle of segregation of duties? Because Singapore, where Leeson was based, was a small office and they wouldn't pay for a local financial controller.

Look at the process end-to-end, without artificial distinctions between front and back office. For example, evaluate the effectiveness of a sales function in terms of total cost relative to the results produced. Sometimes the best way to improve effectiveness may be to add front-line people like sales reps who visit customers. Other times it might work better to add administrators so that the front-line people can spend more time in front of customers. The fact is, effective organisations are a judicious mix of front-line and back-office activities. To promote a simple message of 'Front Office Good, Back Office Bad' is simply to substitute slogans for thought. Leave that to the politicians.

Must Keep Busy

'Dial 1 for customer service, dial 2 to check on progress, dial 3 to be ignored, dial 4 to hear a different useless message . . . your call *is* important to us (that's why we like to keep it on hold for ever) . . . now that you're completely frustrated with us, let us tell you about some other products you could buy from us . . .'

We're all familiar with this. In my case, it's the reason I have moved from being a £900 per quarter customer of BT to being an ex-customer. Why do they do it? Because they have to keep the call centre busy. It's the old National Health Service principle: the doctors' time is so valuable that they cannot, even for a moment, be left with nothing to do. There always has to be a queue of patients. So we wait. And wait. And wait.

This obsession with keeping resources busy doesn't just annoy customers (including some like this *Management Today* columnist who has the opportunity to vent his frustration to 100,000 senior decision-makers on a monthly basis). It has other negative effects as well.

I once worked for an auditing firm that was obsessed with its utilisation rate, i.e. the number of times they were booked for work. The problem was, they looked at this over a year, and auditing is a very seasonal business. Keeping the number up over the year meant being grossly understaffed in the busy season. One alumnus described working there as being 'as stressful as the Vietnam war'. Staff turnover was alarming, and as for quality of work, well, I wouldn't have bought any shares in their professional indemnity insurers.

Keeping busy also stops you thinking about what's happening around you. That's part of the attraction if what's happening around you is scary. Was GM so very busy producing cars that they didn't have time to deal with the fact that people preferred not to buy them any more?

The answer is to put the horse in front of the cart for a change. Look outwards not inwards. What comes first is happy customers and happy staff, then efficiency.

Persistence Pays

Well, maybe it does, and maybe it doesn't. 'Wait!' a self-help guru will cry. 'Of course it always pays. Let me tell you about someone/me who had sent a book to 99 publishers and had it rejected, only to have it accepted by the hundredth and become a best seller'.

Oh, but let *me* tell you about the 100 idiots, and then let's see whether your story is so impressive.

Once upon a time there were 100 idiots who all set out to become rich, doing idiotic things. Ninety-nine of them quickly went bust and were never heard from again. The hundredth, thanks to sheer dumb luck, did become very rich. He then began a lucrative second career as a motivational speaker and self-help author, telling people how to become rich.

Social scientists and statisticians know all about this – it's called survivor bias. It's also, incidentally, why, if I wanted to, I could very easily establish myself as an expert in treating depression. I would recruit 100 patients and prescribe anything – cold baths, a daily diet of sheep's testicles and brown bread, or coffee enemas (sorry if you're reading this before lunch, but I'm not making this one up – I overheard a conversation in a health food shop). Then pretty soon I would have about 30 enthusiastic testimonials to the efficacy of my treatment. This is not the placebo effect, but simply the result of a simple fact. About 30% of cases of depression 'spontaneously remit', i.e., go away of their own accord.

The point is that 'it worked for these people' is no proof that it worked at all. The effect could be random, and unless you know how many people tried it, the fact that there are some happy customers means nothing.

So when does persistence pay? There are some instances.

You could persist with an objective, but be flexible about how you achieve it. Edison famously conducted more than 500 experiments before coming up with the electric light bulb that worked, but these were 500 different experiments, not the same experiment repeated 500 times. The same applies to the would-be author mentioned just now. If you have sent your book idea to ten publishers and none is interested, then rather than thinking, 'Must keep trying, there are another 90 out there' you might do better to conclude, 'I need a better idea.' This book, for instance, didn't go to 100 publishers. The 'Don't You Believe It' column in *Management Today*, which is where this book had its genesis, was the second or third idea I pitched to them. When we came to do the book, the proposal went to not more than three major publishers before being snapped up.

You could persist in looking for good ideas that are easy to sell, rather than persist in forcing a poor, so-so or ordinary idea into the market. Put another way, if you have a square peg and you discover that the world is made up of round holes then throw away the square peg and design a really superior round one. Look around you. Google and Facebook are very persistent in improving their offerings, but there is so much more to it than that; their success owes a huge amount to the fact that they are very good implementations of very good ideas.

THE SIX PILLARS OF REALLY BAD IDEAS, OR HOW TO SORT THE WHEAT FROM THE CHAFF

All of these maxims need to be applied with care. Although some of them should never be applied, most could on occasions be helpful. On other occasions, though, they could be disastrous. The onus is therefore on us to decide whether we can apply a principle or not.

In applying our judgment, let's recognise that a maxim could appeal to us for two reasons:

❶ It's a good idea in the current circumstances.

❷ It appeals to something deeper in us, something we don't fully recognise, independent of the current circumstances. This is a dangerous situation, as it can lead us to conclusions and actions that aren't appropriate.

There are six main ways in which a bad idea can be appealing:

❶ Magical thinking
❷ Feelgood factor
❸ Moral superiority
❹ Fundamental attribution error
❺ Complexity avoidance
❻ Uncertainty avoidance

Magical Thinking

This goes back a very long way. It is deeply rooted in the caveman psyche, and still persists in us today. The caveman had no idea of science or logic, and could only rely on magic to explain much of what went on around him in an incomprehensible world. Any time we are drawn towards an idea along the lines of 'Just do this thing, do it hard enough and long enough, and you will get what you want,' we are experiencing the pull of magical thinking. If we are told that doing A will inevitably produce B, but offered no explanation of the mechanism, then what we are being offered is magical.

Feelgood Factor

Some ideas make us feel good and some don't. Some ideas make sense rationally and others don't. What's important to understand is that these two attributes are independent. Things that feel good, or feel right, may make sense rationally or they may not. By 'make sense rationally' I mean 'will work in reality'. One way to look at this is via the consultant's favourite tool, the two-by-two matrix:

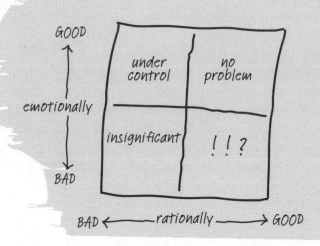

If something makes sense and also feels good you will do it, and there is no problem. Similarly, if something makes no sense rationally and also feels wrong, then you won't do it and that is no problem either.

The other two quadrants are the interesting ones. In the top left, the things that feel good but don't make sense are the impulsive acts. Mostly we manage to keep these under control to the extent that we avoid impulsive actions which damage us. The problem is things we do that aren't exactly damaging in themselves, but distracting and timewasting. This is the story of time management, as discussed extensively earlier. We lose ourselves in valueless activity which feels good as a way of avoiding the really tricky isues, the ones in the bottom right quadrant. These are the things which make sense, or may even be necessary, but feel emotionally wrong. This area will always be a struggle. We will never definitively win the struggle, in the sense that we will never reach a point where the right thing to do always feels right. We need to be constantly asking ourselves what is in our bottom right quadrant, and how to deal with it.

Moral Superiority

Feeling morally superior is a very pleasant sensation, and there are plenty of ways of achieving it at work.

We might work harder than others. Long hours are associated with virtue, which can lead us to do some rather strange things. I once had a job with an oil company where my principal task was to streamline accounting procedures. I met one accountant who on a particular day each month had to come in at 7 a.m. to collect a printout from a process run overnight, enter the numbers into a spreadsheet and then put the results of the spreadsheet into the computer so that another process could run shortly after 9 a.m.

It was obvious to me that this task could be easily automated so that he didn't need to get in early, but he seemed strangely reluctant to discuss this. I also noticed that the spreadsheet was very badly designed which meant it took much longer than necessary to use; in some cases he had to key in the same number in three different places, which rather missed the point of a spreadsheet. Finally, and this was where I almost fell off my chair in surprise, he told me that in fact he only needed to input a dozen or so figures to produce the result that was needed for 9 a.m. The rest he could have done later.

At this point it became clear. Getting to the office at 7 a.m. had nothing to do with getting the job done, but was a way of feeling virtuous. I saw him sitting there at 7.30, hammering away at the spreadsheet, feeling so superior to all those lazy stay-a-beds who weren't going to start drifting in for at least another hour. My code is rather stricter. I don't think you achieve virtue by making things harder than they need to be. In fact, I think it's wrong to do so. The reason is that if you make things harder for yourself you are almost certainly making them harder for others as well.

Sometimes we might feel virtuous by taking bigger risks. This is quite common in literature aimed at entrepreneurs. Taking huge risks is good. It shows courage. Myself, I see the taking of unnecessary risks, or risks that aren't fully thought out, or risks that aren't managed, as just stupid, not virtuous.

The final, rather insidious, form of moral superiority is attributing different motives to others than you do to yourself. You are slow responding to emails from customers and clients because you are terribly busy with really important work; they are slow responding to emails from customers and clients because they are lazy or disorganised. If you deliver something and it's not what they asked for it's because they didn't explain themselves clearly. If someone delivers something to you and it's not what you asked for it is because they didn't listen or don't care.

Fundamental Attribution Error

I have discussed this in the first chapter, but here is a reminder. When we see people doing things we don't approve of, or not doing what we want them to do, we have a powerful unconscious tendency to explain their behaviour in terms of 'That's just how they are' – lazy, ignorant, bloody-minded – rather than 'Given the situation they are in, what they are doing is perfectly reasonable.' This bias predisposes us towards 'solutions' involving changing other people – training them, motivating them or even terminating them – rather than changing the organisational structure, the incentive they have or the information they receive.

Complexity Avoidance

Complexity is annoying, and can be really worrying. You are trying to solve a problem or get something done, but you are struggling to understand the full complexity of the situation. Actions you take don't have the results you expect, and you suspect that you are missing something. As the pressure increases, so does the temptation just to cut through the complexity and *do something*. The problem is that if you don't engage with the complexity of the situation then whatever you do to affect it won't produce the result you want. Ideas that promise simplification are therefore highly dangerous. Simplicity is good, but distinguish between the simplicity which lies on this side of complexity and the simplicity which lies on the far side of complexity.

Uncertainty Avoidance

Complexity, when you know the question but it's hard work to find the answer, is difficult. Uncertainty, when you don't even know the right question, is far worse. Deciding whether to start operations in France today is complex. You know what the key questions relate to – the market, the competition, the customers' perceptions, the overall prospects for the economy etc. Some of these are hard to answer, but you can work through them and arrive at a reasonably robust conclusion.

Deciding whether to start operations in the former Soviet Union in, say, 1991 just after the fall of communism is different. That's uncertain. What is the USSR? Will it remain an empire, or fragment? What is the legal system going to be? Will there be a legal system?

Strategic questions generally tend to take you at least some way into the realm of uncertainty. A lot of the skill in thinking strategically is finding the right questions to ask. There are so many that could be asked, some of them obvious and some of them not, many of them relevant and many not. Sometimes it might be best to start asking questions about products or services: which do we want to develop, which should we be phasing out? At other times asking about products or services may not be helpful and we should ask about customers first. Who do we really want to be serving? Who are the customers who really like our offering and see it as superior to that of our competitors? Once we are clear on that, the question of what products or services to offer becomes much easier. At other times the best question to begin with might be what particular skills we have as an organisation. If there is something we are really good at, we can look for markets – combinations of customer and product or service – that fit our distinctive skills.

How do you become more comfortable, or at least less uncomfortable, in situations of complexity or uncertainty? I wish I had a sure-fire answer, but I don't. The best I can offer is some suggestions:

Recognise where you are, and that different rules apply in different places. However hard it is, accept that, particularly in uncertainty, you can't move with the same level of confidence as you can in more clear-cut situations.

Don't think that more data will necessarily help you. Sometimes the only answer to a question is: 'We can't know (yet).' If that is the case, gathering more data won't help. It could even be dangerous if it leads you to forget about the essential nature of uncertainty.

Spend as much time, if not more time, identifying the questions you need to ask as in trying to answer them.

CHAPTER 7

INCENTIVES

WHEN DID WE BECOME COIN-OPERATED?

The fact is, we didn't. Over the last few decades, as more and more emphasis has been placed on financial incentives as a way of producing peak performance – performance-related pay, share options, the ever-increasing level of senior management bonuses – over in another corner of the world something else was happening. Social scientists, in a series of fiendishly ingenious experiments, were finding out what actually motivates people. The results have been often surprising, sometimes shocking. Perhaps the most shocking thing of all, though, is how unsuccessful the social scientists have been at communicating their findings to business people who could make use of them.

Financial Incentives Don't Ignore Other Sources of Motivation, They Destroy It

Nobody would dispute that there is a whole range of reasons why people want to do a good job, beyond the chance of earning a bonus. These include:

- *Social pressure*: the desire not to let down colleagues.
- *Competition*: the desire to look good, and/or to be recognised as the top performer.
- *Intrinsic satisfaction in the work*, whether it's a nurse helping patients recover from illness, or a software developer creating really cool products.

❍ *Non-financial recognition*, in the form of awards, respect of your colleagues or simply thanks.

Nobody would dispute any of these; most of us are seeking at least some of them, and most of us use them to some extent when managing others. What is less well known is that financial incentives destroy or reduce the effectiveness of these other incentives. Let the social scientists explain.

Two researchers, Uri Gneezy and Aldo Rustichini, studied a kindergarten in Israel. The kindergarten closed at 4 p.m., and parents were expected to collect their children by then. If they didn't, one of the staff had to stay late to look after the kids.

For the first four weeks, the researchers recorded how many parents arrived late. Then they made a change, and introduced a fine. If you didn't arrive by 4.10 p.m., you had to pay a fine of 10 shekels (at the time, equivalent to $3). What effect did this have on lateness? It *rose* steadily, finally reaching a level almost twice that of the period before the fine was introduced.

How do we explain this apparently bizarre and totally counterproductive outcome? Actually, it's easy once we abandon 'logical logic' and engage with psychological logic. Stop assuming that the parents are rational economic actors, i.e., coin-operated automatons. Look at them as human beings with a range of motivations, some of which are stronger than others. In the initial period, there was no fine, but there was a very powerful other motivator to arrive on time: the desire not to inconvenience the staff. Parents arriving late felt guilty, and so tried hard to be on time.

Introducing the fine changed all this. It removed the guilt. The parents saw it simply as a fee for an additional period of child care. Think about it – when you arrive late and have to pay 10 shekels, would you rather explain it to yourself as 'I have done a bad thing and am being punished with a fine' or 'I am taking advantage of an option for extra service'? There is no contest.

Now extend this logic to the employee offered a bonus. The message is: 'Make an extra effort, do the very best you're capable of, and we'll pay you extra.'

This can be interpreted one of two different ways:

- 'Peak performance is an option. Deliver it and you'll be paid more,' or
- 'If you fall short of peak performance you will be punished (by having part of your remuneration withheld).'

If you are the employee, which interpretation would you opt for? Obviously the first. Who wants to set up a situation where they could be punished by being bad? This then creates the chance for the employee to respond: 'Thanks for the offer, but I'm fine with my basic salary. Keep the bonus, and I'll just deliver an OK or mediocre performance. And by the way, thanks also for letting me forget about all those other reasons why I might want to work harder.'

The bottom line is this: reinforce financial incentives, and you will diminish others. So you had better be sure that the financial incentives are big enough to work. The bad news is, in most cases they don't work.

How Financial Incentives Drive Performance – Downward

This is the story. Researchers invented a simple logic problem involving a candle, a box of drawing pins and a book of matches on a table. The task was to find a way of fixing the candle to the wall so that it didn't drip wax on the table. People tried pinning the candle to the wall, but that didn't work. Then some of them tried running the molten wax down the side of the candle and using it to stick the candle to the wall. That didn't work either. In the end, most people found the solution: take the drawing pins out of the box, pin the box to the wall and stand the candle in it.

The subjects were divided into two groups. They told one group that they just wanted to time them to establish norms for the puzzle. They offered the second group financial incentives – the fastest 25% would get $5 and the fastest person that day would receive $20. (This was decades ago, so these were significant sums.) How did the two groups perform? The incentivised group took on average three and a half minutes longer to find the solution.

Why did the incentivised group take longer? It was because solving the puzzle involved a tricky cognitive manoeuvre, that of overcoming 'functional fixedness'. You had to stop seeing the box as a container of drawing pins and see it as a candle stand. The effect of the incentive was to narrow the subjects' focus. As they concentrated more on solving the problem, they missed the idea of giving the box a different function. The candle problem seems like a trivial problem, but it involves a very important ability. Whether you call it lateral thinking, creativity, ingenuity or resourcefulness, it's a very important component of success in most businesses (in most jobs above the purely menial), and was damaged by the financial incentives.

To confirm this conclusion, the researchers repeated the experiment with a small but crucial change. They used the same equipment and the same incentives for the second group, but this time they took the drawing pins out of the box and just put them on the table. This completely changed the problem. The functional fixedness issue disappeared. With this new, much simpler problem the effect of incentives changed. The incentivised group now performed better. The conclusion to be drawn from this is that for very simple tasks, incentives do improve performance. For anything involving thought, lateral thinking or creativity, they damage it.

You can see how this mechanism operated as a major contributory factor to the banking crisis of 2008. Huge financial incentives, both to individuals and institutions, narrowed everyone's focus. All the participants were so intent on creating and selling esoteric securities that nobody stopped to ask where it would all end up.

All this leads to a rather alarming conclusion. Who are the people who most need to use creativity, lateral thinking and ingenuity, who have to look beyond what is currently happening in the business to what could be?

Top management, of course.

They are the ones whose performance is most likely to be reduced by financial incentives, and they are the ones who usually have the largest incentives. Conversely, it's the ones doing the routine jobs, like the assembly line workers, who would benefit from larger financial incentives.

INCENTIVES CANNOT HANDLE COMPLEXITY

In one company I worked with, I found the purchasing manager about to place an order for four years' worth of stock of one product. That is to say, the quantity she was ordering was four times what she was expecting to sell in the next year. This was pretty odd, even if you believed the sales forecast (which I didn't) and even if you assumed that the product would keep selling at the same rate for the next four years (which was at best doubtful). It was even odder given that the company's policy was that any stock at the end of the year in excess of one year's future projected sales was to be written off. Even had the forecast been right, at least half of what she was ordering would be written off at the next year end. Oh, and another thing – the company was desperately short of cash, which was another reason for not investing in stock which wouldn't, in the best of all possible worlds, turn into cash again for four years.

'Why are you doing this?' I asked.

'That's the minimum order quantity,' she replied. The Chinese supplier wouldn't supply in smaller quantities.

That was the answer she gave, but what she should have said was: 'My objectives are to get the lowest possible unit cost, and to make sure that products are always in stock. That's what I'm judged on, and what determines my bonus. The best way for me to meet my objectives is to order from China, where the products are cheapest, in very large quantities. Nobody asked me to think about the cost of the stock writeoffs I generate, or the amount of cash that my decisions consume (despite the fact that the company is way behind on payments to its suppliers, and at least once a week someone from the factory comes into the accounts department saying they need a cheque immediately, as some machine is broken and the supplier won't send anyone to fix it until they have been paid).'

So in fact, her behaviour made perfect sense, within the framework she had been asked to make decisions in. Imagine how different her thought process would have been had it been her own business: 'The supplier wants me to buy four years' worth of stuff? He seriously expects me to commit cash, which I am really short of, to buy things that I can't turn into cash for *four years*, if ever? Never mind accounting policies, will this product still be selling in four years' time? I wouldn't bet on it, even if I had the money. I need to have a serious talk with him about these minimum order quantities. If he won't be sensible I'll need to find someone else, even if they are more expensive. Or if I can't find someone who is more flexible on order quantities, I might have to drop this line altogether. That's not ideal, but it's not a huge seller, after all.'

There is a difference between thinking like an employee and thinking like an owner, but there is another difference between the two thought processes here which is even more important. In her job as purchasing manager, she should be maximising availability or minimising cost. In the alternative, 'owner' way of thinking, the priority is balancing. In this situation there are three things to be balanced:

❶ Unit cost – to be kept as low as possible.
❷ Availability – keeping the goods in stock.
❸ Cash conservation – not tying up huge amounts of money in stock.

If you just focus on the first two, the task is relatively straightforward and you can set about single-mindedly maximising availability and minimising cost. The way to do it is to find the cheapest supplier and order in the largest quantities.

Once you bring cash conservation into the equation, however, the task changes. It doesn't get a little harder, it becomes completely different. It's one thing to maximise – it needs a certain level of technical skill in choosing suppliers, or negotiating. It's another thing to balance – that requires judgement. If your task is to use your negotiating skills to get the lowest price, it's relatively easy to see whether you've done well or not. Once you move on to tasks involving judgement and balance, the whole question becomes more subjective. Yes, you've achieved a certain balance of conflicting factors, but how do we know that you've achieved the best possible result? It's far from clear.

This sort of trade-off abounds in organisations, and very often incentive schemes result in it being handled very badly. Another company I worked with was a magazine publisher. Its advertising sales force had been very strongly incentivised to generate revenues. Nothing unusual about that, you will say. Unfortunately, nobody had mentioned the importance of getting decent rates. If you are under pressure to get a sale, and you are struggling, one of the first things you think of is a price reduction. And then another, and then another. Every time you offer a discount, you just whet the customer's appetite for another. This month's amazing-never-before-seen-never-to-be-repeated special price becomes next month's starting point for a further downward negotiation. But, hey, who cares, because I'm making my revenue numbers, and that's what they want me to do.

In this publisher, matters had arrived at the point where they were selling advertising for 20% of what their competitors were charging. That's five pages from us for the cost of one page from a competitor. It had gone so far that even the customers realised something was wrong. When a newly appointed advertising director started visiting them to explain that rates needed to start rising towards sane levels, she got responses along the lines of, 'Fair enough, we did think it was getting too good to be true.'

Here again, it is a question of balance. I could close a particular sale by giving an extra discount, but against that I need to balance the fact that I am filling the magazine with unprofitable advertising, and setting expectations, not just of this customer but of others, for future sales.

There are many, many more trade-offs that need to be made in organisations, and balances that need to be struck and maintained. Here are some examples:

- Promises made on delivery dates to secure the sale versus cost of meeting those promises (or not meeting them).
- Speed of fixing customers' problems versus cost of fixing them.
- Cost of salary rises versus risk of losing key staff if they don't get a rise.
- Future benefit of product development or market development versus current cost.

Now, you could argue that there are stupid incentive schemes (like that of the magazine publishers, based solely on revenue), and sensible ones that do produce the desired results. I would argue, though, that in many situations, including most of the important ones, incentive schemes won't do the job. The candle problem explains why this is. Remember the conclusion of the candle experiment? If the task involves any sophisticated cognitive activity (as in that case, overcoming 'functional fixedness' to see the box of pins not as a box but as a candle stand), then financial incentives narrow your focus and make you less effective. If doing my job well involves achieving a balance between conflicting factors, then a financial incentive will narrow my focus and make me less effective. If I am a banker, for instance, the chance to make a huge bonus by dealing in esoteric securities will blind me to the issue of risk, or even to the fact that I don't have a clue how to value the securities I am trading.

It's clear that the further up the organisation you go, the more time managers spend, or should be spending, on questions of balance – sales vs profit, current profitability vs growth, cost vs quality etc. Further down the organisation, it's more likely that people just need to maximise one thing. Or is it? It's interesting to look at some 'shop floor' level jobs and think whether in fact the workers should just be thinking about maximising one thing. Take, for instance, refuse collectors – you might think the key factor is simply to get round the collection route as fast as possible. But wait – there are other factors here that are worth considering. You need to work safely, which isn't always compatible with maximum speed. Then there are the quality issues – make sure you take everything, don't leave refuse scattered over the front garden or the pavement . . . Even at this very lowest level, there are trade-offs to be made.

So how to deal with the problem of balance? How do you make sure that people do what is best for the organisation as a whole? Is there some sort of more sophisticated financial incentive you could introduce? I don't think there is. For a financial incentive to work, there needs to be a very clear link between what you do and what you receive, and in this case that's impossible. The results of the organisation are the result of the actions of many different people in many different areas, and it is impossible to disentangle the whole to allot praise or blame to individuals.

You need a different approach – education. Rather than say, 'You're not bright enough to understand the situation of the business as a whole. You just concentrate on maximising x and y and let us worry about the big picture,' give people credit for being able to understand more. Put differently, assume the responsibility for helping them to understand more. So to the purchasing manager you say, 'We need to balance profit (achieved through low unit cost), product availability and cashflow. How do you think we can best do that?'

There is evidence from the recent financial crisis which suggests that a knowledge of the big picture does result in people taking better decisions in complex situations. As most banks, driven by the prospect of apparently huge profits and bonuses, loaded themselves up with ever-increasing quantities of ever more toxic securities, one bank stayed largely aloof. That was J.P. Morgan, and the reason that this is interesting is that they were the ones who had invented most of those securities in the first place. Several times they looked at what their competitors were doing and asked themselves the classic big picture question: 'How can they possibly be making money doing that?' The bankers at J.P. Morgan couldn't answer that question, and so stayed out of the market.

Digression: How Do You Design an Incentive Scheme for Picasso?

This question is more relevant than it might at first appear. What it really means is, how do you develop incentive schemes for people when you don't even know what you want them to do, but you need them to do great things, to step beyond what has been done before?

Consider Picasso, indisputably one of the greatest artists of the last century. What made him great?

▶ He kept changing throughout his career.
▶ He came up with ideas, ways of seeing, that nobody had ever seen before.
▶ Nobody, probably not even he, knew what he was going to do next.

How would you design an incentive scheme for this man?

▶ You can't reward productivity. I can produce scribbles at the same rate, or faster, than Picasso could, but that doesn't make me a great artist.
▶ You can't define his output – '100% bonus if you invent Cubism' – because *he* needs to think of that. Until he has done it, you don't know that that's what you want.
▶ You can't offer him more money if his work sells for more; if he cares about money, which he probably didn't much, that would incentivise him to keep repeating what worked. Social scientists also dealt with this one. They had a group of observers assess paintings which artists had done to commissions against those that they had done for themselves, and found the commissioned work to be inferior.

When you look at it this way, you see that Picasso's attributes are valuable across a very wide field. For anybody building a business, or taking it through significant change – which probably includes most people running a business – they are crucial. You can't just copy what others have already done. You need to keep coming up with new ideas, even when you have no idea what they will be. Note that this imperative doesn't just apply to top management building the business. It applies to anyone who could, if they wanted, use their intelligence to find a better way to do their job. That's find a better way, not just work harder.

Financial incentives don't look like a very clever way of doing this. There had better be some superior alternative.

Fortunately, there is. One organisation which has addressed this issue is Google. They famously let their programmers spend 20% of their time doing anything (software-related) that they find exciting. This doesn't just help Google recruit the best people, but has produced significant new products such as Google Mail.

INCENTIVES REDUCE COOPERATION

Think about it; how much can anyone actually do in an organisation without support and cooperation from other people? Almost nothing. And yet incentive schemes are designed as if each individual can control their own results. It makes no sense, and can positively undermine performance.

I once worked for a marketing consultancy which had an office in the UK and an office in the US. Each office looked after its own market: the UK people sold projects for European programmes to clients based in Europe, while the US people did the same thing for clients based in the US. They were effectively two separate firms. We realised, however, that we were missing something. The clients were global corporations, and sometimes they wanted a marketing consultant with global capabilities. If we could get the US and UK working together, we could bid for some very large contracts indeed.

We appointed a very senior (that is to say, very expensive) Director of International Business Development, gave him a huge budget for travel and entertaining, and waited excitedly. Nothing happened. Lots of travel, lots of activity, but no contracts signed. What we hadn't done was look at the incentive schemes operating in the different offices. For our international guy to be effective, he needed a lot of support from others. People in the UK and US needed to give him access to their clients. He needed staff to develop the very elaborate presentations we used to win business. Neither of these was forthcoming, for a rather simple reason. The individual offices were principally incentivised on the basis of their local performance. If they gave access to their clients, or allowed some of their staff to work on 'international' business, it potentially reduced their own results. They didn't get enough credit for any 'international' business to make that worthwhile.

MOTIVATION, OR METHOD?

It's easy to see problems in achieving objectives as related to lack of motivation. In fact, 'lack of motivation' or 'not trying hard enough' are wonderful one-line explanations of just about any problem. What's even better is that if you are the manager, and you see lack of motivation or lack of drive as a moral failure, it gives you a wonderful warm feeling of moral superiority to apply it to someone else. It's a great way to deal with problems, with only one disadvantage – it often doesn't work.

The reason it often doesn't work is that no amount of motivation or drive will solve a problem of poor method. It helps to think about how to do something before you start to boost the effort.

At about the same time, a friend of mine, Stuart, and I decided that we wanted to lose some weight. Stuart's approach was to hire a personal trainer to put him through some painful routines at the gym. My approach was very different.

I don't like pain, and I particularly don't like paying to have it inflicted on me. I don't like the idea of another fixed appointment in my diary, which is full enough already. Finally, I don't like the idea of one part of me paying someone else to force another part of me to do something it clearly doesn't want to do. That sort of psychological split, I feel, does violence to something in my nature and creates all sorts of stresses and strains that will slow me down in other areas of life.

I needed an approach that worked without will-power. First, I took some specialist advice. My son is a serious athlete; he has competed at regional level in both running and cycling and made a serious study of nutrition. The best way to start the day, he explained, is by exercising on an empty stomach. Because you have no carbohydrates in you, the body burns fat. Then, as soon as you stop, have a protein shake. This alters your metabolism so that you feel less hungry for the rest of the day. This suited me fine, as I was already starting the day by cycling to work. The first protein mix I tried tasted disgusting, but I was able to find one that was actually quite pleasant.

The next step was to observe what I was eating over the rest of the day. A quick study of the calorie count of my usual office lunch showed that I could eliminate 500 calories by cutting out the packet of crisps and fruit drink I usually had, and choosing a different sandwich. The final step was to develop the habit of eating some dried fruit in the middle of the afternoon so as to avoid getting too hungry before dinner.

The result was a dietary regime which involved no extra expense, no extra time commitment, no pain and no self-denial, but which enabled me to consistently lose a kilo a week. Would it work for you? I have no idea, but this isn't a book about weight loss. The point is that method can be a better alternative to motivation. I can understand how Stuart might get a warm, virtuous feeling from all the pain he's suffering, but I get a greater satisfaction from having found an ingenious, painless solution.

For another illustration of this principle, go to your local swimming pool on any weekday morning. You can usually see someone, and it's usually a man, battling his way up and down like a mini-tsunami, arms and legs flailing, water splashing all over. And then there's someone else, usually a woman, doing an apparently effortless front crawl, slicing through the water like a knife, *doing about twice the speed of the mini-tsunami*. Technique matters. Get the method right before you turn up the motivation. If you get the method absolutely right, you might not need the motivation at all.

The dieting example just applied to me as an individual, but it also applies to organisations.

I worked with a software company which had severe, long-standing problems collecting money from customers. It had been poor at this for years. From time to time it had made spasms of activity to reduce the problem, but the results, if any, had never lasted more than a couple of months. The issue had become sufficiently serious to become visible to the chief executive. His take on the matter was very simple: the credit controllers and accountants needed to work harder. Apply bigger sticks and carrots and the results would come.

Examining the situation more closely, it became clear that things were not as clear as they had been presented. Almost all the outstanding monies due had one of three stories attached to them:

- ◗ *Software does not perform in accordance with documentation.* The OMGEO gizmo doesn't interface properly with the FX wotsit. What is a credit controller supposed to do with this? It is the development department who need to deal with it.
- ◗ *Dissatisfaction with professional services.* 'Yes, Fred was on site for 20 days, but we don't think he knew what he was doing. He should have done the job in 10 days, and that is all we will pay for.' Again, a credit controller can't deal with this. We need the professional services department to get involved.
- ◗ *Can't understand the invoice.* 'We have five agreements signed at different times, each with an annual

maintenance charge. You have sent one invoice for the whole lot, and we can't relate the total to our contracts.' Here the contracts department needs to get involved.

So it turned out that the company could have had unlimited numbers of credit controllers working 24 hours a day, but they couldn't have solved the problem. It was a question of organisation: getting the right people working on the problem. Once they did that, the problem of slow payment went away and didn't come back.

The point in both these cases is that applying the motivation solution rather than improving the method creates strain. In the case of my diet, the most important point was that *I didn't have any motivation to spare for losing weight.* I was writing this book, which requires serious amounts of self-discipline. Every morning I needed to sit down in front of a blank sheet of paper or a blank screen, ignore all distractions, and create. My willpower, like everyone else's, is a limited resource. Some of us have more than others, but nobody has an infinite amount and if we use it in one area, like losing weight, it's not available for use in other areas, like handling difficult or unpleasant tasks at work.

Similarly, in the case of the software company, shouting at the credit controllers to work harder, or increasing the carrot and stick (maybe by tying the carrot to the stick and hitting them harder with it), just wouldn't get the job done. The system was broken, and the responsibilities were in the wrong places. Until that problem was solved, extra effort would just create extra stress and strain.

The difficulty with seeing 'motivation' as an answer to common problems is that it is a one-size-fits-all solution. If we assume that doing something is necessarily going to be painful, require lots of effort or be difficult, we are creating a self-fulfilling prophecy. Applying the motivation solution first blinds us to the particularity of the issue.

What exactly is the problem? Where are the points of leverage, the points where the smallest effort could have the biggest impact?

YOU CAN'T INCREASE MOTIVATION . . .

. . . you can only burn it up faster.

This is another problem with motivation. Even once we have fixed the method, we can't assume that extra effort or motivation will solve the problem. It might, if we could find it. But often we can't.

There is certainly evidence that self-control is a limited resource, as some social scientists established in another entertaining experiment. The research subjects were led into a waiting room. On a table at the front of the room was a bowl of delicious-smelling, freshly baked cookies, and a bowl of radishes. Half the participants were asked to eat some cookies but avoid the radishes, while the other half were asked to eat radishes but avoid the cookies. The experimenter then left the room. This was a severe test of self-control for the radish-eaters. Nevertheless, they managed to resist temptation (as verified by a hidden camera). Then both groups were asked to solve some logic puzzles. The puzzles were in fact insoluble; the experimenters wanted to see how long the subjects would persevere. It turned out that the cookie-eaters stuck with the task for an average of 19 minutes, while the radish-eaters gave up, on average, after 8 minutes. Why did they give up sooner? Because they had used up their reserves of self-control resisting the cookies.

Once you start to see motivation, self-control, self-discipline, or self-supervision as a limited resource, things start to look very different. It's like muscle power. You have a certain amount, but when that amount is used up you need time to recover. You can make a sudden huge effort in an emergency, like when a piano falls on your foot and you somehow find the superhuman strength to lift it off, but you are not creating any extra power, just using what you have more quickly. If you really overstrain yourself, something breaks for good.

Suppose that what holds true for muscle power also holds true for motivation. When we 'increase our motivation' for a task, are we actually increasing it, or just burning up our existing stock more quickly? I suspect the latter. Are there things we can do to increase our stock of motivation, the same way we can build muscle power over time? Maybe, but I haven't a clue what they are. Zen Buddhism, tantra, yoga, esoteric martial arts? I have no idea. What we hear from motivational speakers or writers seems to be much more along the lines of 'burn it faster [but don't ask what to do when it's all gone]'.

This leads us to a very profound change of perspective. If you find yourself suffering from 'lack of motivation' or even 'lack of self-discipline', it is not, as currently conceived, evidence of some sort of moral failing or character defect. Change your perspective, and the result will be liberating.

For a start, you could stop castigating yourself for being lazy. So you didn't take ten minutes this evening to clean the kitchen after you had cooked dinner? Such a trivial task? Well, yes, it's a trivial task, but if you have used up all your self-control at work, or on some new extreme exercise regime, then you won't be able to do it.

Let me hasten to say that this isn't an argument for never cleaning the kitchen – you will have to do it from time to time to prevent it becoming a health hazard. It might be an argument for paying someone else to clean the kitchen, but more than that it's an argument for thinking hard about what you do with your motivation. If little things like spending ten minutes with a cleaning cloth are becoming hard, your reserves of motivation are probably running dangerously low. Where is it going? Are you making the best use of it? What happens if another challenge appears over the horizon? How will you deal with it? What needs to give?

After that, you could think about budgeting your motivation. Do you do this? No doubt you budget time, and you budget money. You know that you don't have enough of either for everything you want to do, or that other people want you to do, and so you make decisions about where time and money are best spent. You probably don't do that with motivation. You tacitly assume that motivation is unlimited, or that failures of motivation are moral failures rather than practical problems, like the battery of your laptop running down while you are on the train. If you believe that, then budgeting for motivation, and recognising that it is a finite resource, is either pointless or immoral.

WHY ALL THIS MESS ON INCENTIVES?

If you accept even some of what I am saying about the ineffectiveness, or counterproductiveness, of incentives, the obvious question is, why? Why are so many people getting it so wrong?

The reason that the use of financial incentives is so problematic, and creates so many problems in organisations, is that they try to reduce complexity by more than is possible. It violates Einstein's dictum that 'Things should be made as simple as possible, but not simpler.'

These are the areas in which the use of financial incentives tries to achieve a simplicity which is just impossible to attain:

◖ It reduces the complexity of human behaviour to a simple 'coin-operated' model of individuals. Simplicity is a virtue, but realism is a greater one. Look around the world, and look at your own behaviour. Can you see people doing things for non-economic motives? It seems to me that the decisions driven by economic motives are in the minority. Mostly, we do things because we want to look good, or feel safe, or enjoy the approval or respect of our peers, or have fun, or learn new things. When you look at life as a whole, this is hardly controversial, but we seem to have an inhibition about recognising it within organisations.

◉ It ignores the complexity of organisational life. The truth is, let's admit it, that there is very little anyone can do in an organisation without the support and cooperation of others. Fundamentally, business is a team game. And yet, we give incentives to individuals, for individual achievements. Why? Because it's simpler.

◉ It ignores the complexity of the decisions people make, and the subjective nature of performance. Any job above the simplest is not about maximising something, but achieving a balance between conflicting objectives.

Digression: Scientific Management

'Scientific management' is straight out of the Cemetery of Dead Ideas. The problem is, it's like a vampire that won't stay in the tomb. Every time somebody drives a stake through its heart (it has been comprehensively discredited and abandoned in manufacturing, for example), it rises again somewhere else.

It's a 100-year-old technology. The basic ideas go back to Frederick Winslow Taylor and his 'scientific management' ideas from the first years of the last century. The basic premises of this, paraphrasing but not fundamentally distorting, were like this:

◉ We, the managers, are clever.
◉ You, the workers, are stupid.
◉ We will therefore design your tasks for you; what you do, and how you do it.
◉ You, workers, will do just what you have been told to

do, in the way that you have been told to do it. Concentrate on doing it as fast as possible.

● As a further guarantee of peak performance, we will set up a series of rewards and punishments for you.

Sound familiar from any organisation you know? Any call centre you have recently dealt with? Do you enjoy dealing with call centres? Remember the story about 'Dell Hell' from Chapter 4 on measurement? It's a classic case of Taylorism rising from the tomb to wreak havoc with its narrow-minded and stupid obsession with the length of a call. Remember that F.W. Taylor, working about 100 years ago, was organising and codifying what was then working. So it's likely that what he came up with is what worked up until then. What has changed since? A great deal, but perhaps most importantly of all, whereas in Taylor's world most people could be 'workers' and it was enough just to have a few 'managers', today almost everybody needs to behave like a 'manager'. Everybody needs to be looking for better ways to do things. Everybody needs to have some view of the big picture. This means, going back to the candle problem, that almost everybody is trying to solve the difficult version of the problem, the one with the tricky cognitive manoeuvre, not the simple one. Incentives, therefore, are getting in their way.

In my career I made this rather humbling discovery. For years, I made something of a speciality of 'turnaround' situations. I was there because my predecessor had failed and the company was in a serious mess which needed to be resolved very quickly. In this sort of situation you have no option but to do what works, regardless of whether you or anybody else thinks it 'should' work. What I discovered was that, no matter how chaotic things were, people doing the job had a better idea of how to do it than I did. This applied right through the hierarchy, from qualified accountants to teenaged clerical staff. I was hugely more experienced than they were, but the less I interfered with the way they did their work, the better the results. My job was to make sure they understood the objectives, and to give them feedback. I would in effect tell them: 'You know these ten priorities you had? Forget seven of them, and concentrate on these three.' Then I would make sure they knew how well they were doing, with daily updates on amounts of cash collected, or numbers of customer disputes resolved, or whatever else the priorities were. I didn't think about 'motivation'. I didn't offer financial bonuses – I couldn't, because there was no money available to do so. Despite the surrounding chaos, almost everybody became highly motivated. Most people do, when they know what they need to achieve and how well they are doing it.

SOME 'MOTIVATIONAL' STRATEGIES THAT DO WORK

❶ Recognise the complexity of individuals. This might not be a welcome message, but you might as well recognise the reality; people are complex, varied in their motivations and sometimes perverse. It's a cop-out to treat them all as rational economic actors.

❷ Recognise the interconnectedness of organisational life. Don't set individual incentives where results arise from a team effort.

❸ Don't fixate on 'motivation'. Think first about method. If you want performance to rise, start by assuming that people are already trying their hardest. They might benefit from training or coaching, or a reorganisation of the work, or a clearer understanding of what the organisation is trying to achieve. Doing this is a little more complex than simply applying bigger carrots or bigger sticks, but on the other hand, it is more likely to work.

❹ Recognise the complexity of the decisions people need to make. Like the purchasing manager, they need to make subtle trade-offs between conflicting objectives. You don't know if they have achieved the best they can – you don't even know what the 'best' result is. How can you possibly set targets for an incentive scheme?

Get beyond Taylorism. Stop telling people: 'This is your job, and these are your objectives.' Instead try: 'This is what we are trying to achieve, and this is how we are doing. What can you do to help?'

WHY YOU CAN'T DISPENSE WITH BONUSES

Given all this bad news on the malign effect of financial incentives, it might be tempting to get rid of them altogether, but this won't work either.

To understand why, we need to go to one of the furthest corners of the Cemetery of Dead Ideas and exhume the work of Karl Marx.

Marx thought a lot about what he called 'surplus value'. The idea was that value in business was created by the efforts of the workers, but the wicked capitalists managed to capture a lot of that value, effectively by paying the workers less than the value of what they actually produced. The capitalists could do this for several reasons:

- ● They had the upper hand, as capital was scarce, and workers were plentiful. There was a 'reserve army of labour', i.e., unemployed workers living on nuts in the jungle, ready to take the jobs of any workers who declined to play the capitalists' game.
- ● Workers were quite interchangeable. Your typical 19th-century factory worker or miner didn't have much in the way of education or specialised skills. They offered muscle, not brain, and that is not hard to replace.
- ● The structure of 19th-century industry favoured the capitalist. The value was in the capital investment, not

the workers. If all the workers in a mine or factory left, the value remained in the factory or mine. The workers couldn't do much on their own, and the capitalist could easily recruit a new group of workers. Contrast this with a more typical modern business, say for example an investment bank. Here it is very easy for individuals or teams to jump ship, and in this case they take the value – knowledge and client relationships – with them. Their old employer is left with very little.

Marx's solution to this was that the workers should take over the means of production. This led to some spectacularly ineffective and inefficient forms of economic organisation, maintained, as in the case of the former Soviet bloc, by some exceptionally unpleasant political regimes. Nobody wants to go back there. It's over, thank God. What actually happened was different, and much more interesting.

The workers didn't take over the means of production. The workers *became* the means of production. It's not a question of 'our people are important to the business'. It's a question of 'the people *are* the business'. A great many employees intuitively understand this now, and are acting accordingly, as I did fifteen years ago.

I had the opportunity to become Finance Director of a substantial design agency. The agency was owned by two people. One of these, the Commercial Director, was driving the recruitment. He had actually been a marketing director and a client of the agency before moving over. His reason for the move was that he saw huge unexploited potential in the agency; with a more commercial focus, it could grow revenues and grow profitability very substantially. He had been there several years and become very frustrated. The potential was still there, but he had not been able to realise it. He felt that getting the right finance director was an essential part of the plan. I agreed with him, and saw how I could improve results dramatically by doing the same as I'd previously done in another creative agency – and make the two owners several million pounds richer.

Given the value of my contribution, it seemed reasonable (to me, at least) that I would be given a share of the equity. Why would I want to spend my time slogging away to make two colleagues millions of pounds richer, in return for just a reasonable salary? A Marxist would say that I had 'achieved revolutionary self-consciousness'. I would simply say that I understood my value and my self-respect would not allow me to settle for just a salary and annual bonus.

As it turned out, they were very unreceptive to the idea of the equity stake, and I ended the discussions. I don't think the equity stake would have made me work any harder had I taken the job. Like most people who work at senior levels, I am driven by very personal factors to do my best. What would have killed me, had I taken the job without the equity stake, would have been the perceived unfairness. I would have been working as hard as my colleagues to make them, and not me, rich. It would have wrecked my relationship with them. I have made plenty of stupid choices in my career (some of them, if there were a Hall of Fame for Daft Decisions, would be right up there with Napoleon invading Russia), but this one was obvious even to me.

SO WHAT *DO* YOU DO ABOUT INCENTIVES?

We have arrived at a point where we can't live with them and can't live without them. We need them if we want to be able to recruit good people, and we need them because we need to maintain a sense of fairness when it comes to financial reward. On the other hand, they can produce so many unfortunate results. What can you do? Here are some suggestions for at least a partial solution to the problem.

Accept that only a partial, or good enough, solution is possible. This is probably good advice for dealing with any of the issues in this book, but in this case it is crucial. The whole point of incentives is that they work on human psychology, and the whole point of human psychology is that it is perverse, contradictory, paradoxical and generally bizarre and infuriating. No incentive scheme can fully deal with this, but you could drive yourself mad trying to. In particular, avoid increasing complexity. It is easy to get into the vicious circle where a particular scheme leads to unintended consequences, which lead to fixes to the scheme, which lead to more complexity, which lead to more unintended consequences, which lead to more fixes, which lead to more unintended consequences... which leads ultimately to a system that nobody understands and whose results are wholly unpredictable and divorced from what you were originally trying to achieve. Keep it simple.

So far as possible, rely on non-financial incentives. Pride in the job, delight in personal mastery, desire to support colleagues and look good to them ... these are all powerful factors which can be nurtured to drive performance. Remember how introducing financial incentives on top of them will destroy them. Look for people who seem driven by these factors. Someone who seems driven by a desire to surpass themselves or be part of a successful team is probably a better hire than someone whose principal interest is in their own financial reward – you can spot this at the recruitment stage. In most jobs, someone who appears excessively 'coin-operated' may well end up trying to maximise their own personal reward at the expense of colleagues or the organisation's purpose, and that is *not* what you want.

Reward team success with team incentives. Who in your organisation can be successful without the support of others? Who doesn't have a way to boost their own results in ways that create problems for others? There are not that many. Mostly, teams succeed or fail together. It's good to remind everyone of this, and if you do use financial incentives they must support this. It's no good talking about team effort if you pay individual bonuses.

Don't expect the paying of bonuses to boost performance. Financial rewards can persuade people to join you, and the right arrangements can take the subject of money off the table so that people can get on with their jobs without being troubled by a sense of unfairness. Financial rewards won't, in most cases, improve performance. For that you need something else (hint: it's called management).

Maintain fairness. This is a vital point. There is good evidence to suggest that money doesn't boost performance, but a sense of unfairness in the way it is distributed will reduce it anyway. More and more, the people you want will see themselves as independent means of production. In a way that Marx might enjoy (or might be appalled by), they have liberated themselves mentally from the proletariat and started to think like capitalists. It's not good enough to offer them the going rate for the hours they put in – they will want a share of the value they create.

Educate people. Stop shutting them up in silos with the instruction to concentrate on their own tasks and let you look after the big picture. Help everyone to understand how their individual task contributes to the whole. Give them the information they need to understand how that whole is doing, and how what they do helps or hinders. This can be powerfully motivating, provided you don't then mess it up by offering narrowly focused financial incentives.

Ask what *you* add as an employer. There is a temptation to build businesses by simply buying in the top performers, but this runs into several problems:

- The stars turn out to be mediocrities who are good at personal PR and selling themselves at interviews.
- The stars were genuine stars in their last place of employment but aren't effective in their new habitat.
- The stars do excel in their new habitat, but in line with

the neo-Marxist analysis above, capture all the value of their performance for themselves.

The really important question you need to be able to answer is this: 'Why will these people be more productive working for us than for anyone else?' It's a simple question to ask, but hard to answer. If you don't have a decent answer, however, it will make no sense to employ them.

The 19th-century coal owner or factory owner may have taken a lot of flak from Marx and others of his ilk, but he did at least have a good answer to this question. Without the mine or the factory, the workers would be reduced to digging in their back gardens with shovels or weaving on handlooms in their attics – that is to say, completely unproductive.

The 21st-century business needs to come up with a similar answer to the question. It probably isn't as simple as owning the mine or the factory. It may involve proprietary technology or sophisticated equipment, but increasingly it is going to have to be something involving the way people work together. It could be culture, or a better-designed organisation, or a clearer, better communicated sense of where the business is going which motivates and directs its staff.

CHAPTER 8

IT'S TIME TO START THINKING ABOUT THINKING

ARE YOU FEELING PARANOID YET?

I hope the previous chapters have not left you depressed or despairing. I do hope, though, that they've left you productively paranoid. I hope that I've planted in your mind a seed of doubt, an idea that you may sometimes be misleading or misdirecting yourself.

Keep the paranoia to a low level. There is an answer.

How to Get Your Thinking Out of the Cave

First, recognise how caveman thinking is condition-ing the way you deal with modern problems. In particular, recognise that the caveman deals very badly with change.

Second, use the rest of the book to help you spot areas where your thinking can be upgraded.

The good news is that you have all the tools you need. You need to practise them more consciously, and train yourself to spot when the caveman is interfering. That involves *thinking about thinking*.

THINKING ABOUT THINKING

Let's distinguish three levels of thinking, each with an associated picture.

The first is the simplest:

This is the reflex action, also known as the conditioned reflex or, even less charitably, the knee-jerk reaction. There is a stimulus – something we see, or hear, or smell – which produces a response. The same stimulus, experienced 100 times in different places, or in different contexts, will always produce exactly the same result. The process is unconscious; although we have in fact made a decision, we're not conscious of having done so. We haven't considered alternatives.

This approach was popular in the Stone Age, and with good reason. Most threats or opportunities were the same as ones encountered before, they weren't hard to recognise or understand, and the action required was simple. 'See the big sabre-toothed tiger – run!'

The great advantage of the reflex reaction is its speed, and the fact that it *feels right*. The caveman might have worried about whether he could outrun the sabre-toothed tiger, but he wasn't troubled with any doubts as to whether running was the right thing to do.

There is neurological evidence, based on brain scans, that we take many decisions before we think about them. That is to say, the decision-making parts of the brain activate before the verbal parts. When we think, we believe that we are making the decision, but in fact we are rationalising what we have already decided. As one social scientist put it, 'Human beings are not rational beings, but rationalising beings.'

To illustrate the point, consider this very simple puzzle. A racquet and ball together cost $1.10. The racquet costs $1 more than the ball. How much does the racquet cost? You probably jumped to the wrong answer: the racquet is $1. I did, and *I am a maths graduate*. The answer 'racquet is $1' jumped into my mind, from where I have no idea. Then the mathematical part of my mind jumped in and said something like, 'Hold on, that's not quite right . . .'

In the end I had to use algebra to work it out:

$$r + b = 1.10$$
and
$$r = b + 1$$
so
$$2b + 1 = 1.10$$

thus
$$b = 0.05$$
and
$$r = 1.05$$

This is a trivial little problem, albeit fiendishly well designed to mislead. Almost getting it wrong gave me a moment of amusement, but imagine what would have happened had I encountered a similarly misleading problem while trying to land an aeroplane.

Business abounds in questionable reflex reactions:

- ▶ Departmental performance is slipping. Somebody is not up to the job. Either get them some training or fire them.
- ▶ Profits are down – costs need to be reduced.
- ▶ Sales are slipping – our prices are too high.

As we'll see, these are at best highly questionable responses. Most of the time, they are just plain wrong.

So much for the reflex reaction. The next level up in sophistication comes the algorithm, or checklist.

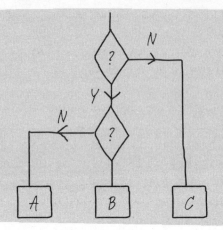

Unlike the reflex reaction, this works on the conscious level. Something happens, and you run through a decision process:

◐ It's a sabre-toothed tiger.
◐ Is it a very big one? If yes, run.
◐ If no, do I have my spear with me? If yes, fight it. If no, run.

In the modern world, this could be applied by a pilot experiencing engine failure:

◐ Has the engine just stopped, or is it on fire?
◐ Am I within reach of an airport, or am I over the middle of the ocean?

This type of thinking is more sophisticated than the conditioned reflex for several reasons:

◐ It actually stops to examine the precise nature of the stimulus (big sabre-toothed tiger or small one, engine stopped or engine in flames?).
◐ It looks at the context (do I have a spear with me, am I within reach of an airport?).

- ◗ It allows for different responses depending on the first two points.
- ◗ It is conscious – we know we are taking a decision as we work through the algorithm.

The disadvantages of the algorithm are twofold.

First, it is slower than the reflex. In certain situations you may not have time to evaluate the exact nature of the stimulus (it's dark, I can't see how big this thing is, but it has lots of teeth and is making nasty hungry-tiger noises . . .). Sometimes there may simply not be time get the data, or to think it through.

Second, it requires the situation to be relatively clear cut. You may not know things, but you know what you need find out. The choices of action need to be relatively clearly defined and few in number. This is quite feasible for a pilot flying from London to New York, but less so for a chief executive piloting a complex business through a recession.

The algorithm can't deal with fuzzy questions like, 'What should this business look like in five years' time?' Neither can it deal with the 'unknown unknowns' – the things we don't know we don't know.

Consider how we could apply an algorithm to the reflex reactions mentioned earlier:

- ◗ Departmental performance is slipping. Somebody is not up to the job. Either get them some training or fire them.
- ◗ Profits are down – costs need to be reduced.
- ◗ Sales are slipping – our prices are too high.

Stop and reflect on this thinking. Is the reflex approach the right one for solving these problems? For example, what could cause sales to be declining? High prices are certainly one possible cause, but what else could it be?

What is the necessary timescale for solving these

problems? It's not seconds or minutes, as it is for the caveman meeting the tiger or the pilot with the burning engine. The actions required to solve these problems will be taken – will take effect – over months or even years. It shouldn't therefore be a problem to take a few days or even weeks to work out exactly what the problem is and run through the options for solving it.

Wherever you look, you find examples of decisions taken as reflex actions that would have been better had they been taken using an algorithm. Take two examples:

At the start of the recession in 2009, different packaged goods firms produced very different results. Procter and Gamble saw profits reduced by 18% while Unilever saw a 17% reduction. Reckitt Benckiser, on the other hand, saw profits increase by 14%. The difference was accounted for by the fact that the first two appeared to succumb to a reflex reaction, while Reckitt went through a thought process.

Unilever and P&G thought, 'Tough times ahead, consumers want to spend less.' They introduced 'value' versions of their products.

The Reckitt thought process, on the other hand, was more sophisticated. They thought, 'Tough times ahead, consumers will become more conscious of value. Either they will want to spend less, or we need to work *harder* to persuade them that it's worth spending more.' Reckitt chose the second option, introducing substantially superior versions of its products, in some cases costing twice as much as 'budget' versions. Because these versions were genuinely superior, they were successful, and Reckitt's profits rose.

The second example is from my own experience. A client asked me to visit their Spanish subsidiary, which was really struggling. They had almost decided to close it down and do their best to serve the Spanish market from France. I went through the thought process described in Chapter 3 on cost cutting, and found that in fact the company was a growth opportunity.

The Four-Level Problem Solving Model

Before we move on to the third form of thinking, let me offer you a useful general-purpose algorithm, the four-level problem solving model. This is a way of, very quickly, considering all the possible reasons for a problem and thereby making sure that you identify the real cause and so come up with an effective solution.

The first step in solving a problem is to understand where the cause is located, which can be at different levels in an organisation. For example, if you are worried about increased pricing pressure, giving your sales force negotiation training isn't going to help if you are trying to compete on price with the Chinese. This model is to help you be sure that you have located the real problem, and are not just dealing with a symptom.

The model uses a hierarchy of four levels. Generally, when a mistake is made about the location of the problem, it is usually put too low rather than too high. Interventions made at higher levels usually have greater impact. Problems at a higher level can make intervention at lower levels ineffective; in the example below, if the company's product is obsolete or too expensive, no amount of work on sales incentives or selling skills will produce an improvement.

The four levels are, in descending order:

❶ *Strategy and objectives*: what is the product, who is the customer, who is the competition? How large is the company?

❷ *Organisation*: who is responsible for what? How is authority delegated through the organisation? Is this completely clear? Are there any overlaps or gaps?

❸ *Incentives and information*: what are the incentive arrangements (informal as well as formal)? Do they support the overall aims of the organisation? Is information available to show how well the organisation is progressing against its strategic goals?

Individual performance: questions of skills and motivation.

The following table shows how the same problem, 'sales are too low', can be located at different points. Each location needs a different solution.

Level	Example for problem 'sales are too low'
Strategic	• We are selling steam trains • We are trying to compete with the Chinese • Our revenue budget is £50m, our competitor's marketing budget is £40m (i.e., we're too small)
Organisation	• Field force trying to sell to individual stores in chain – need a national accounts function • Several sales staff calling on same customer selling different lines
Incentives and information	• Don't know who our best customers are, so can't identify high potential prospects and prioritise accordingly • Informal incentives based on activity rates rather than results • Lack of data on total customer relationship (e.g., bank cannot identify when savings scheme customer is same person as mortgage customer) • Low or non-existent incentives for cross-selling
Individual performance, motivation and skill	• Sales staff cannot articulate USP or value proposition • Sales staff demoralised • Sales staff poor at negotiating with aggressive buyers

Using the model, you can quickly identify what is going on, and what needs to change. For instance, I used it with a managing director whose problem was 'department managers are not controlling their overhead costs sufficiently tightly'. We went through the four levels:

- ◗ First, strategy and objectives. In this case it's objectives; do they all understand that it's their job to control their overhead costs, and do they realise how important that job is? Hmm . . . maybe not in all cases.
- ◗ Second, organisation. In this case, the question is whether it is clear who is responsible for what. If there are costs for which nobody is really responsible, or costs where responsibility is shared, you are less likely to get good control. Here, everything is fine.
- ◗ Third, information and incentives. Do all the department managers get the information they need? Is it sufficiently detailed? Yes and yes – no problems here.
- ◗ Fourth, individual performance and skill. Do all the managers have the financial knowledge they need to make sense of the cost reports they get and work out what to do? Some of them probably don't.

Now we have the prescription for action. Talk to all the managers and remind them that controlling overhead costs is an important part of their job. Then arrange some tutorial sessions with the finance department so that everyone understands how to do it.

This took about five minutes to do. Once you ask the questions, the answers are easy to find. The value is in going through a process which forces you to look at areas which you wouldn't otherwise notice. In this situation I would probably have missed the possibility that some of the managers didn't know how to interpret the reports. That's because I have a financial background and see these things as absolutely elementary. Someone else might have missed the fact that nobody had communicated to the managers just how important it was to control overhead cost.

There are other useful algorithms around. For example, Michael Porter's Five Forces Model is a very useful algorithm for thinking about strategy. There is a risk when doing this of focusing on the existing product range and the existing competitors. Porter's model forces you at least to consider whether there may be other players about to enter your market, and whether there may be substitute products which might capture market share. It won't take decisions for you, but it will help you take better decisions.

The two methods discussed so far, the reflex and the algorithm, will deal with most of the decisions which come up in normal life. There are some cases, however, which need something more powerful.

This is creative thinking.

Creative, or 'Messy', Thinking

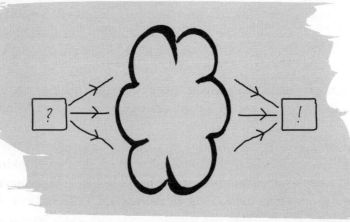

The picture for this is much messier. You have an initial question, and a range of ways of proceeding. In the middle of the picture is a cloud, or a fog, of uncertainty. You move through the fog (in a way that the diagram does not begin to explain) and then converge on an answer.

This is the sort of thinking you need when the question

is loosely defined, such as: 'What should this business look like in five years' time?' and you don't even know the questions you need to ask to start with.

There's quite a lot not to like about this way of thinking, at least for most people.

- There's the fog of uncertainty in the middle. What's in there? How do I navigate through it? Will I in fact be able to navigate through it, or will I get lost for ever in the middle of it, possibly travelling in a circle?
- It's difficult to put a timescale to the thought process. With an algorithm you know what the steps are and the order in which you go through them, and so can plausibly claim to be 50% or 75% of the way through the process.
- If someone else is relying on you to solve a problem this way and they're at all anxious, it's going to be difficult for you to reassure them. If you had an algorithm, you could at least explain it to them and keep them updated on progress through it. You could say something like, 'We have identified the root causes and are now evaluating three different possible solutions. We expect to have a recommendation by the end of the month,' which is much better than 'We are in the fog of uncertainty and hope to emerge from it some time, somewhere.'

The good news is that, for most situations, creative thinking isn't necessary. You can reap the benefit of past experience, or the experience of others, by using an algorithm.

The bad news is this:

- For some issues, creative thinking is the only solution, and
- These tend to be the most important issues, the ones that make or break your business.

How Can You Decide How to Decide?

All three types of thinking have their uses. The point is to make sure that you choose the right one for the right purpose. It would be stupid to go through a creative thinking process to solve a problem that has been solved many times before by you or other people and could be dealt with by means of an algorithm. On the other hand, it would be futile to try to apply algorithms based on past experience to a question which is entirely new, where it's not clear what information you need, or what is the root cause of what you observe. That requires creative thinking, whether you like it or not.

Note a couple of features of the different types of thinking, which will tend to colour your decision of which to use, not necessarily in helpful ways.

Reflex action is very fast. If nothing else, it lets you move immediately to action. If you are under pressure from above, from your boss or from your investors, to produce a quick response, a reflex action is very appealing. It's also appealing if you are under a lot of time pressure yourself. An algorithm can be very fast (for example, a pilot planning an emergency landing) but it will usually take longer. It needs some investigation before you decide what to do and implement. Creative thinking is longer still, and what's worse, the timescale is unpredictable.

Reflex action feels comfortable. It feels 'right'. We aren't really aware of taking a decision at all, so all the business of uncertainty, error, regret or embarassment if we get it wrong just doesn't apply. Using an algorithm is conscious. We are aware that we are taking a decision, and that we might get it wrong. On the other hand, the algorithm gives us comfort. It gives us confidence that we have at least asked all the right questions, and if the worst comes to the worst, gives us cover. We can always justify ourselves – we followed the process. If it didn't work out, there must have been something exceptional at work. Creative thinking doesn't offer this sort of reassurance. You are on your own, and if it goes wrong there's nobody else to blame.

So allowing for this bias, how do you decide how to decide?

Reflex action works when it doesn't matter what is causing the effect that you see. If I observe X, it doesn't matter whether X is caused by A, B or C. Whatever the cause, the necessary action is the same.

The algorithm, on the other hand, is needed when you need to investigate causes. I observe X. If it's caused by A, then I need to do Y. If the cause is B, then I need to do Z.

Take the example given earlier. Suppose that profits are down. A reflex action is to cut costs. An algorithm might lead you to consider two causes. Maybe it's because costs are too high, in which case you do indeed need to cut them. On the other hand, maybe it's because prices are declining as a result of competition from the Far East. If that's the case, then cost cutting probably isn't the answer.

Creative thinking is the last resort when the issue isn't sufficiently clear cut for any of the other two methods. It tends to apply to the big questions, like: 'Should we still be making these products at all?' or 'What does this business need to look like in five years' time?'

Try an Experiment

Observe yourself thinking for a week. How many decisions do you take using the different methods?

● How many decisions do you take as a reflex, moving straight from problem to solution?

● How many decisions do you take using some sort of algorithm? You may not consciously move through a series of questions, but if you ask yourself what could be the possible causes of what you observe, or what could be alternative courses of action, that is what you are doing.

◐ How many decisions do you take using the creative thinking process?

Now ask yourself a few questions:

Where did I take a reflex decision when I could have, or should have, gone through an algorithm? Were there cases where I jumped from problem to solution, when more investigation would have helped?

Conversely, were there cases where I went through an algorithm when I didn't need to? Are there types of decisions where I think the decision through in stages, but always arrive at exactly the same answer? Could I stop thinking in these cases, and just react?

Where have I applied the creative thinking process? Did I need to? Could I reduce the decision to an algorithm?

If I didn't use the creative thinking process at all, why was this? Remember that the creative thinking process is very often the one needed for big, important decisions about the future. Can it be true that there is nothing like that going on? Or am I missing something?

So, taking all this together, and recognising that every form of thinking has its value – am I applying the right one in the right situation?

We are now halfway to liberation from worn-out thinking. We have covered the rational part. Now it's time to move on to the emotional part.

CHAPTER 9

WHAT TO DO NEXT

LIBERATION

If you have reached this point in the book, it must surely be because it has struck a chord. You have seen you or your organisation falling into some of the traps I have described, and you would like to do better.

You now have the tools, but even if you have a very clear idea of what you want to change, the battle is at best half-won. You can see the changes you want to make, but making them could turn out to be the most difficult part of the process. Resistance will emerge.

That is why this chapter is mostly about psychology, particularly your own. You are going to have to deal with your inner caveman, with his particular way of looking at things. As you start to think unfamiliar thoughts and do unfamiliar things, you will feel resistance. You will also need to deal with social pressure. Remember the psychology experiment with the three lines in Chapter 1. You will find yourself, repeatedly, in the position of the research subject who thought they were almost going mad. It was obvious that line B was the same length as the line on the right, so why is everyone else saying it is line C?

Give Yourself Permission to Be Human

This is probably the single most valuable thing you can do. As you begin to take action, strange things will probably start to happen. It should be clear by now that all of us have minds made up of different parts, all working in different ways and pulling us in different directions. We have the power of logic, reasoning and planning. We have intuition. We have the caveman's atavistic fear of anything new and a shared tendency to knee-jerk reactions. We have blind spots, irrational fears, cognitive biases which prevent us from seeing how things actually are, and inexplicable resistances.

There are different ways of dealing with this, and two common ways of getting it wrong. Sometimes we decide that we are just fine, and that all our mental apparatus is perfectly adapted to our situation. The way we see things is the way they are. Our split-second decision about what to do is necessarily right. More than that, our split-second method for taking decisions is right in all cases.

The other wrong way to deal with our flawed humanity is the way of the motivational speaker. We accept that we are screwed up – irrational fears, avoidance, procrastination and resistance – but decide to fix it (by which we mean ourselves) all in one heroic act of will. This whole business of motivation has become a huge industry, but I suspect that it has reached the size it has for the same reasons as time management has: that it basically doesn't work.

Giving yourself permission to be human would mean giving yourself permission to be imperfect. Giving yourself permission to be human would also mean extending the same courtesy to others. Once we abandon the idea of perfection in ourselves, we can also abandon the idea that others should be perfect. This has two liberating effects. Our collaboration with others becomes much less stressful, and also more effective. When somebody doesn't react in the way we expect, instead of dismissing it as personal failure or deliberate obstruction on their part, we try to understand it.

There's No Such Thing as 'Irrational Behaviour'

This may seem a very strange thing to say in a book about abandoning pointless, unproductive ways of doing things, but the best way to deal with stupid behaviour is to assume that no behaviour is stupid. Stupid behaviour exists for a reason. We have seen many examples through the book of how perverse incentives, lack of information or inadequate organisational structure result in people, inevitably, doing things that don't achieve the organisation's objectives.

The next time you see someone doing something which you think is stupid, don't assume that it's because they are stupid. Instead, ask yourself a question: 'In what circumstances, with what understanding of the situation, with what incentive structure, is that sensible behaviour?'

Remember the distinction between logical logic and psychological logic. Your default assumption is very probably that reason should prevail, but that isn't going to be the case. Don't see this as a problem, but see it as a huge opportunity. Remember also the psychology of pricing, and how a pricing scheme for magazine subscriptions, which made absolutely no sense whatsoever in logical terms, produced great results in practice.

Dismissing behaviour as irrational is a way of saying, 'I don't understand, and I can't deal with this.' It's essentially a counsel of despair, and most of the time there's no cause for despair. Apparently irrational behaviour is explicable once you have identified the mechanisms going on. Think of business as an orienteering contest, where you need to move through a complex, unfamiliar landscape with the aid of a map, and keep ahead of your competitors. The map in this case is the set of assumptions and beliefs which you use to predict what will happen and what others will do. The map also determines how we interpret what we see. Taking a more sophisticated view of what drives behaviour is like getting a better map.

I'm Biased, and That's Fine

It's fine because I *know* that I'm biased, and can adjust for it. I can't eliminate all my various mental biases without ceasing to be human, but fortunately that's not necessary.

All of us have biases which affect what we see when we look at a problem. I often notice others falling into the Fundamental Attribution Error (FAE) – assuming that people behave the way they do because 'that's the way they are' when in fact it's the system in which they operate and the incentives they are given which make it inevitable that anyone would act that way. The reason I notice the FAE so often is because I have the opposite bias. People who know me would say that I tend to look first at systems and organisation as a way of explaining what is going on, at the cost of missing significant facts about individuals. I have to admit that they are often right, but that's fine because I've taught myself to take a second look so that I'm not completely blindsided by the thoroughly bloody-minded individual causing havoc in a perfectly sensibly structured organisation.

The point is that we all have biases, in one direction or another. If we want to improve our chances of finding the right diagnosis or the right response in any situation, we need ways of overcoming them. The previous chapter presented some rational, sensible ones. Now we look at some which work on the emotional level, without which reason does not stand a chance.

Expand Your Comfort Zone

The section in the chapter on time management showed how, so often, we do the wrong things because we stay within our comfort zone. It's time to find the way to move out.

The first step, and by far the most important, is to recognise and accept that we have comfort zones, and that some of what we need to do is currently outside of them. Wherever we are professionally, some of the things that others reasonably expect of us do not feel comfortable to us. Does this worry you? Do you feel guilty about it? If so, give yourself permission to be human and simply accept it. Assume that everyone else is in the same situation, whatever image they may be portraying to the outside world. Drop the guilt, and the problem becomes much more manageable.

Next, work out what specifically is outside the zone that you need, or want, to do. That's not hard once you have accepted the idea that you aren't perfect, that some of the things you find hard are things that others find really easy. Go through the time-management routine to identify the urgent and important items, but this time also note how they make you *feel*.

Now you know what you need to do, and it's time to start gently pushing outside of the comfort zone and do it. The key word is 'gently'. You have to take time. Think of it like climbing a flight of stairs. You might go up one step at a time, or possibly two, but if you try to do ten at a time you will just fall back down to the bottom again. The idea is that, over time, you can make the unfamiliar familiar, and hence unthreatening.

Recruit Some Help

Preferably strange help. Let's go back for a moment to that experiment described in Chapter 1, with the three lines of different lengths. Remember how 75% of the subjects could be manipulated by social pressure into giving an obviously wrong answer? You will have to overcome some strong social pressure if you want to upgrade your or your organisation's thinking. There is some good news from the experiment. A later version of it found that just one dissenting voice among the stooges made it much, much easier for the subjects to give the right answer.

If you can arrange one dissenting voice, you will find it dramatically easier to spot where you are going wrong. If you can arrange several, better still. You will also find that the best people to help you are those from outside your own world. It's unlikely that anyone from your own speciality (finance, FMCG marketing, software development or whatever) will be much help, nor will anyone from your own organisation. As an example, here are the three people who have most helped me over the last year:

- Andy – former lecturer in computer science, NLP practitioner, consultant in organisational development.
- Nathalie – web designer, musician, psychologist.
- Nick – consultant psychiatrist, psychoanalyst, formerly head of a major psychiatric institution.

There are several significant points about these three. It is clear that none of them is from my world. Two of three have very varied backgrounds, combining elements not often found together.

How do you tell who is going to be a good collaborator? There are a few points to look for.

One is that they should have the ability to accept your situation but not be limited by it. Another way of putting it is that they can distinguish between what is genuinely a constraint on you, and what you only think is a constraint.

Good collaborators know when to urge you on and when to hold you back. You will sometimes come up with ideas that seem insane. Some of the possibilities you see will make you fear that you are succumbing to delusions of grandeur. This is when you will need an objective opinion to reassure you that you're not taking leave of your senses altogether.

One of the crucial skills of a good collaborator is the ability to see the possibilities you are missing. Look, for instance, at Charles Babbage, who first had the idea for the computer. His vision was essentially for a large calculator, which could do what it was designed to do. It was Babbage's collaborator, Ada Lovelace, who had the idea of making it programmable. You could build the thing, and then think of other things for it to do. He thought of hardware and she added software. Apply this kind of collaborative approach to your own situation. Look for comments such as: 'I like the article, but I think there is a bigger, more interesting idea lurking in there that you haven't brought out,' or 'If you changed this and this, you would have something that would appeal to a much bigger market.'

When you receive advice, ask yourself: 'Would they say the same to someone else?' This is very important, because the default position of so many people who offer advice is to tell you what worked for them, or for someone else, but which might not work for you. What my three advisers are able to do is to come up with ideas that might actually work for me. They know enough about me to tailor their advice.

Take It Slowly

If you decide that you would like to break away from conventional wisdom and start living more effectively and more resourcefully, you need to recognise that the thinking is the easy part. The emotional aspect will be the more difficult one. You will need to manage with less social support, or organise alternative sources of social support. You will need to engage with some powerful, primitive parts of your psyche.

This is where I really take issue with the motivational gurus and the self-help books. Liberating yourself from worn-out thinking will be a process, not an act. I can't offer you seven steps to anything, nor can I promise that it will all be done in 21 days.

There is no once-and-for-all method for freeing yourself from worn-out thinking. Rather, there is a set of practices for keeping your thinking, and therefore your decisions and actions, in tune with an ever-changing reality, making you a little freer every day, even if you never achieve complete liberation. It will always be worth the effort, and that effort will become less over time.

Don't Try to Start a Revolution

I'd love it if you did, but I must admit that it wouldn't be in your own best interests. I would suggest starting slowly. Look for something that's relatively easy to change, preferably something that only involves you. Most of the ideas in this book can be applied to a whole organisation, but there is plenty that you can apply just to yourself. You don't need to ask for permission. You don't even need to tell any of your colleagues that you have decided to start doing things differently. Just decide where you want to change, make a plan, discuss it with your private advisers if you need to, and make a start.

Conserve Your Reserves of Self-supervision

Remember the experiment with the cookies and the radishes in Chapter 7's discussion about incentives, which showed how self-discipline is a limited resource. You can expand the idea of self-discipline into a more general ability for self-supervision. Self-supervision means the ability to watch yourself as you do something, and when necessary to correct what you are doing. It is crucial when you are learning something new, or moving into new areas. Think, for example, of the huge mental effort involved in learning to drive, having to coordinate a whole range of unfamiliar new tasks. Liberating yourself from worn-out thinking is the same sort of task, and you need to be prepared.

I had this point illustrated in a very surprising way when I started writing this book. I play violin in an amateur chamber music group, but found that when I started the book my playing went to pieces. I couldn't concentrate on the music, couldn't listen to the others playing, couldn't master it, however often we went through it, and stopped enjoying it. I had to stop until the book was finished.

It may or may not be acceptable to you to have your efforts at work impacting on your personal life like this, but it probably won't happen. Writing a book is a pretty huge task. The more likely risk is that you take on too many things at work at the same time. You will need to be ruthless about priorities and think very carefully about what to take on and what to ignore.

Make Friends with Anxiety

A strange idea, perhaps. We tend to see anxiety as a bad thing, but it makes more sense to see it as a valuable signal.

Anxiety is misleading us when it comes from the primitive view that what is familiar is safe, and what is unfamiliar is dangerous. This reflex is left over from the Stone Age, but is still hard-wired into a very old part of our brains. Primitive people didn't have science, or logic, or much language to work out whether an unfamiliar situation was safe or not, and so they fell back on a very simple principle. If something was familiar to them, they had survived it before and so it was safe. If something was unfamiliar, who knew? Best to avoid.

This was an effective strategy in an unchanging world, but it hardly makes much sense now. Imagine applying it in the technology business. Making PCs is familiar, but hardly safe. Cloud computing is unfamiliar, but probably a safer bet for the next few years.

The fact is, any unfamiliar situation will tend to make us anxious. It means nothing beyond the situation being unfamiliar, which is a pretty common occurrence these days. Anxiety here is unhelpful, unless it is of a particular type.

'Signal' anxiety is the sort that really matters. It comes from our unconscious recognising that something new is going on. That something could be good or bad. The message is: 'Pay attention!' but too often we interpret it as: 'Not in a good place, get back to safety.' We may have this reaction even if we are on the verge of a breakthrough.

Concluding, therefore, feeling anxiety might mean:

- We are approaching something good.
- We are approaching something bad.

> ● We are approaching something which is neither good nor bad, just different.

This may seem unhelpful, but with practice we can begin to distinguish the different forms of anxiety and understand what they are trying to say. Anxiety ceases to be an unpleasant feeling, and becomes a valuable sixth sense. You can turn it into a principle. Somebody asked me recently how I decided the first thing to do each day. My answer was: 'The most important of the things I don't feel like doing.'

Three Things to Do NOW (and Forever After)

My agent tells me that lots of people start reading books at the back, and never read more than the last chapter. If you are one of those people, here is what you need. If you started at the front, here is the essence of what you have just read.

In either case, write these three commandments somewhere you will see them every day:

● Think about thinking.
● Give yourself permission to be human (and extend that courtesy to others).
● Recruit some strange help (start spending time with people very unlike you).

Good luck!

BUT THERE'S MORE . . .

If reading this book has left you fired up to upgrade your thinking, I'd like to offer some more help.

For an almost daily feed of new ideas, practical techniques, stimulations or provocations, including a free monthly telephone seminar, subscribe to the *Don't You Believe It* blog at www.dontyoubelieveitblog.com. If Twitter is your preferred channel, follow me there – acddryburgh

INDEX

Note: Page numbers in **bold** denote major subject treatments.